Awakening to Wisdom

Note from the Author:
In 1981 I assumed the name Mariamne Paulus to express my commitment to take my place publicly as a Light Bearer and as a Wisdom teacher. All books written before the year 2001 carried my given and married names. This series on the Wisdom Teachings, however, is published under the name that carries the frequency of the Wisdom tradition and that I use in my teaching.

Books by Diane Kennedy Pike

Four Paths to Union
(as Mariamne Paulus)

Life As A Waking Dream

The Love Project Way
(with Arleen Lorrance)

My Journey Into Self: Phase One

Life Is Victorious!
How to Grow Through Grief

Cosmic Unfoldment

Channeling Love Energy
(with Arleen Lorrance)

The Wilderness Revolt
(with R. Scott Kennedy)

Search

The Other Side
(with James A. Pike)

AWAKENING TO WISDOM

by
Mariamne Paulus

Teleos Imprint ~ *Scottsdale, AZ*

Teleos Imprint
Wisdom Books
Published by LP Publications
7119 E. Shea Blvd.
Suite 109 PMB 418
Scottsdale, AZ 85254-6107

Copyright 2003 by Diane Kennedy Pike
All rights reserved.

The Teleos Institute World Wide Web site address is
http://www.consciousnesswork.com

Library of Congress Cataloging-in-Publication Data

Pike, Diane Kennedy.
  Awakening to wisdom / by Mariamne Paulus.
    p. cm.
  Includes bibliographical references and index.
    ISBN 0-916192-48-2 (pbk.)
  1. Self-actualization (Psychology)–Miscellanea. 2. Religious awakening–Miscellanea. 3. Consciousness–Miscellanea. I. Title.
  BF1999.P5485 2003
  299'.93–dc21
                                         2003008172

First Printing, 2003
Printed in the United States of America

Photo of echinopsis thelegona cactus flower on cover
by Arleen Lorrance

Teleos Imprint
Cascade of Angels

Lily Jean Haddad

DeLorre Haddad

Thomas G. McCarthy

Hollis Johnson

Dorothy Enslen

Vera Isaac

Patricia Elliott

Suzanna Neal

Cathy Young

Would you like to be included in our cascade of angels?
Call 480-471-3082 or e-mail ljh4848@aol.com.

AUTHOR'S NOTE

Special thanks go to **Lily Jean Haddad** for her encouragement to release *The Process of Awakening* in a new form, and for reading and commenting on the manuscript as I worked with it.

To **Patricia Nerison** I owe a great debt, for she helped me enormously with the rewriting and expansion of the original manuscript, carefully noting everything from typos to grammatical errors to nuances of the deepest implications of the content of the text. I am so grateful that she was willing to help me polish this expression of the Wisdom, to which she is also dedicated in her life.

My thanks to **Arleen Lorrance** for brainstorming with me, offering her support, and making suggestions for the improvement of the manuscript.

Thanks also to the Angels who are named on a previous page. Their financial contributions have made possible the publishing of the Teleos Imprint Wisdom Book series.

Finally, my gratitude to Irv Hershman who contributed his skills as a professional indexer to help create the index for this book. He saved me many hours of work, for which I am very grateful.

I dedicate this book

To
Vitvan

whose perception and expression of the Wisdom
have illumined my understanding

and to
Laurel Keyes

who embodied the Teachings and
expressed her confidence in my ability to do the same

They brought the Father-Mother Force into focus for me through their persons, their lives, their writings and their teaching. I consider them to be my spiritual parents. They have been:

Lights to guide my feet along the Path
Lights to illumine my mind
And Fires to warm my heart that I might know God

For the blessing they have been in my life, I am eternally grateful, and I dedicate my life to the Light forever.

Contents

Introduction i

    Chapter One: The Quest 3

Part One: The Theoretical 5

    Chapter Two: The Wisdom Teachings 7

    Chapter Three: The Sacred Science 14
        The Nature of God 15
        The Structure of the Universe 17
        Universal Laws and Principles 21
        The Nature of Humanity 23
        The Purpose of Human Life 26
        Laws and Principles
            Applied to the Human 30
        Secrets of Initiation 32

Part Two: The Practical 33

    Chapter Four: The Process of Awakening 35

    Chapter Five: The Human Sleep State:
        Objective Self-Consciousness 57

    Chapter Six: Phase One of the Awakening:
        Identifying with the Personality 71

Chapter Seven: Phase Two of the Awakening:
Learning to Function Consciously
Through Body and Psyche 94

Chapter Eight: The Transformational Process .. 137

Chapter Nine: Phase Three
of the Awakening: Shifting Identity
to the Real Self 146

Glossary 162

Index 167

ILLUSTRATIONS:

Figure 1: . Objective Identity:
         Personality & Private World 86-87

Figure 2:   The Personality 101

Figure 3:   The Personality
          in Expanded Awareness 130-131

Figure 4:   The Autonomous Field (Real Self) 155

INTRODUCTION

The seed of your real Self[1] was planted long ago in the womb of the Great Mother[2] where it has been slowly gestating over millions of years. Reading this book is an indication that the seed of Self is maturing within you. This description of awakening to wisdom will help you to identify your current phase of unfolding and to discover how you can encourage the natural process of growth already underway within you. You have the potential to become a fine cultivator in your own garden of consciousness.

Much of the material in this book was first presented as *The Process of Awakening*.[3] At the time of that publication (1985) it was intended as an introduction to and overview of a series of books that was to follow. Life intervened and the rest of the series was never published.

In the subsequent eighteen years, I have continued to study and to grow in my own experience of the Wisdom. When it came time to return to the intended series, it seemed only appropriate to rewrite the introductory

---

[1] Whenever I use the word "Self" with a capital "S," I refer to the real Self, which is the One Self in relation to which there is no "other." "Self" with a small "s" refers to the personality (including the body).
[2] For quick definitions of terms like "the Great Mother," refer to the Glossary at the end of the book.
[3] Diane Kennedy Pike, San Diego: LP Publications, 1985.

book. *Awakening to Wisdom* expands the original text by coupling it with an introduction to the Wisdom Teachings (Part One) and by elaborating on the Process of Awakening (Part Two) with examples and further description. The result is a new book.

Since 1970, I have been a devout student of the teachings of an American Master named Vitvan[4] (one who knows) by his teacher Mozumdar. Born Ralph DeBit, he founded the School of the Natural Order[5] to disseminate his teachings, which were a correlation of the Western stream of the Wisdom Teachings with modern scientific findings.

Although I never knew Vitvan in person (he died in 1964), I was close to one of his students, Laurel Keyes,[6] who introduced his teachings to me. From my first reading of *The Christos*,[7] I was thrilled to find someone who could elucidate my own experiences, call into consciousness my intuitive knowing, and point the way for me as I continued my unfolding. Vitvan liked to refer to his teachings as a mental roadmap. That roadmap has served me faultlessly over these years of intense passage through the transformational process described in Part Two of this book. Each time I return to one of his lessons, I find new levels of perception are opened to me, and I continue to be in harmonic resonance with the frequencies in

---

[4] Read *Vitvan: An American Master*, by Richard Satriano, Baker, NV: School of the Natural Order, 1977. Vitvan's own works are available from The School of the Natural Order, P. O. Box 578, Baker, Nevada 89311 or at www.vitvan.org. I especially recommend his book *The Christos*. Though it is not easy reading, it is a comprehensive presentation of the theme I offer in this book. I also recommend the Basic Teachings, presented in three volumes under the title *The Natural Order Process*, and his small books *The Veil of Maya, Perceptive Insight* and *Clear Thinking*. Once

Introduction iii

which he functioned and communicated.

Over the years, I have supplemented my study of Vitvan's teachings with extensive reading of other great teachers such as Sri Aurobindo, G. I. Gurdjieff, P. D. Ouspensky, Swami Yogananda, Swami Vivekananda, Jiddu Krishnamurti, Rudolf Steiner, Dion Fortune, and most recently, teachings offered by the Builders of the Adytum.[8]

In 1982 enough of my consciousness had become identified with the real Self that I felt ready to embark on the task of teaching the Ancient Wisdom to which I was first introduced by Laurel and Vitvan. Since then I have offered regular classes in San Diego, CA, in Scottsdale, AZ, and by cassette, across the United Sates and in Canada. The work has been intense and challenging for me as a teacher. Many who have studied with me have urged me to publish the Wisdom in my own words, which they assure me are easier to grasp than those of many more advanced teachers.

What I offer in this book is a synthesis of what I have learned from the teachers mentioned above and other books I have read. My understanding is informed by my own process of awakening. Of course my ability to present the Wisdom Teachings is limited by my own state of consciousness, and I encourage readers to test my pre-

---

you have read one or more of those, any one of his books or lesson series (available in printed form or on cassette tapes) will serve you very well.
[5] The School of the Natural Order, P. O. Box 578, Baker, NV 89311. www.sno.org
[6] See her spiritual autobiography, *Sundial,* Denver: Gentle Living Publications, 1979.
[7] Vitvan, Baker, NV: School of the Natural Order, 1951.
[8] An inner school headquartered in Los Angeles. See their website: www.bota.org

sentation of the Teachings against your own experience, perception, and understanding.

If in reading you find that you want to know more about a given subject, I hope you will remember that this book is only intended as an introduction. In other Teleos Imprint Wisdom Books, as well as in the many available books by other authors, you will find your desire to know will be nurtured until wisdom and understanding blossom from within you.

I wish you well as you cultivate your own unfolding consciousness. If I can be of service to you in any way, it would be my privilege.

– *Mariamne Paulus*
a.k.a. Diane Kennedy Pike

Teleos Institute
7119 E Shea Blvd. Suite 109 PMB 418
Scottsdale, AZ 85254
E-mail: Teleosinst@aol.com
Website: www.consciousnesswork.com

AWAKENING TO WISDOM

2 AWAKENING TO WISDOM

All of the religions of the world have been built upon that universal and adamantine foundation of all our knowledge – direct experience.
– *Baird T. Spalding*

Chapter One

THE QUEST

At a certain stage in the developmental process, a strong urge to know arises in us. The basic questions of life awaken with a personal force: *Who am I? Why am I here? Does God exist? What is the meaning of life?* The urge to know through personal, direct experience compels us to undertake a solitary quest beyond group identities, beliefs, and guidelines into the individualizing process. This is the beginning of the spiritual journey.

The quest to find our own way inevitably leads us to the Wisdom Teachings. Sometimes we find a teacher who seems to speak directly to us. We may find a book, or a book may find us. Perhaps a seemingly random comment resonates with our inner core. The contact, however it comes, awakens in us a feeling that we have come home.

On first acquaintance with the Wisdom Teachings, our personalities are often thrown into turmoil. They do not have enough information to be able to surrender to this inner journey. Questions plague us. We feel disoriented and perplexed. What is going on? Why am I drawn to this person/book/teaching? What *is* the Wisdom? And what is the individualizing process?

Many people have expressed their bewilderment to me over the years. This book is my introductory answer to their questions. It provides an overview. Other Teleos

Imprint Wisdom Books offer a more complete response that will be more satisfying and gratifying. This introduction puts the other books in proper perspective. I hope it will serve to orient the reader to the path that lies ahead. Moreover, I hope it will awaken a hunger for deeper understanding and a thirst for knowledge through direct experience.

– Mariamne Paulus
Scottsdale, AZ
March, 2003

PART ONE

THE THEORETICAL

Chapter Two

THE WISDOM TEACHINGS

Since before recorded human history, a group of teachings that presents universal truths about the nature of the universe and humanity's place in it has been available to the spiritual seeker. These truths express the perceptions of those who have fully awakened. Such men and women have, through their own direct experience, seen through the misleading impressions and beliefs that most of us accept as our everyday reality. They have consciously registered the energy world in which we live, that world of particles, atoms, waves, and frequencies which modern physics is exploring with great dedication.

The remarkable and wonderful thing is that these awakened Beings, no matter what their background, culture, or period of history, have all seen the same essential reality. Their experiences are universal. The truths they express have been tested again and again throughout history by other spiritual seekers and have been found to be sound in the most fundamental way. Even modern physics has begun to confirm their perceptions.

The thread of these universal and eternal truths has been consistently woven into the heart of every culture and every religion. Often, however, those who had no experiences of direct perception and who tried to grasp the truths with their ordinary consciousness have distorted the meaning of those truths. Thus what we have been taught in our religious and philosophical upbringings has not adequately prepared us to undergo the individualizing process.

Fortunately for us, the original Teachings have remained intact in nearly all cultures. They have been called the Ancient Wisdom, the Ageless Wisdom, the Perennial Philosophy, the Gnosis (which means directly perceived knowledge), Theosophia (Greek for Divine Wisdom), Brahma Vidya (the Wisdom of Brahma), and, simply, the Wisdom Teachings.

Where Can We Find The Wisdom Teachings?

There are two primary streams of Wisdom Teachings, one in the East and one in the West. The Eastern stream has many branches, the largest being the Vedic philosophies (based on the sacred books called the Vedas and the Upanishads). The philosophy and practices of Yoga is another branch of the Eastern stream, one that has become widely available in the West. Buddhism in its several schools also holds the Wisdom Teachings. And finally, the philosophy of the Tao, which arose in China and merged with Buddhism in Japan to form Zen Buddhism, presents the Teachings in simple, paradoxical aphorisms. These traditions have had an unbroken continuity for thousands of years, in spite of conquering armies and cultures. They are readily available today to students from both the East and the West, though it is important to find teachers who know *through their own experience* the keys to the Wisdom.

The Western stream of Wisdom Teachings surfaced first in Egypt before and during the time of the Pharaohs over 5,000 years ago. During thousands of years, up to and including the time of Jesus, people traveled from great distances to be initiated into the Egyptian Wisdom. Then, as initiates, they carried the Teachings back to their own people where the Wisdom was passed on in various forms. The Hebrew Kabbalah made the Egyptian Wisdom available within the Jewish culture. The Pythagorean Schools, the Greek Mystery Schools, and the philosophies of Socrates and Plato, were expressions of the Egyptian Wisdom within the Greek culture.

Why Haven't We In The West Heard More About The Wisdom Teachings?

For thousands of years the Wisdom was taught only by word of mouth from teacher to student in both the East and the West. That oral tradition has continued in the East right up to the present. Spiritual teachers have been held in high regard and cultures have supported those who seek out teachers for spiritual instruction. The modern exception is China where the atheist orientation of Communism nearly eliminated cultural regard for spirituality in the 20th Century and individual expressions of spirituality are now viewed with suspicion.

In the West a great change came about in 380 A.D. when the Emperor Theodosius established Christianity as the state religion of the Roman Empire. Once the Christian Church became identified with the secular state, both Christian secular rulers and the priestly hierarchy began to persecute anyone whose teachings seemed to contradict the doctrine adopted by the Church.

In response, the Western stream of the Wisdom, including the Kabbalah, went underground to survive. Only traces of the Wisdom Teachings remain in Christianity itself, primarily in Biblical texts where they are veiled by symbols, myths, allegories, and parables.

Within the Church, those who awakened to a direct experience of the Wisdom were called Christian Mystics. To keep them isolated from the general public and from most believers, Church authorities relegated them to cloistered lives as monks and nuns.

Why Are The Teachings Given In Symbolism That Seems So Difficult For Us To Grasp?

Both Eastern and Western teachers of the Wisdom have used symbolism, myths, allegories, and parables to convey their understanding of fundamental truths because didactic words are so inadequate. Words communicate in the three-dimensional realm. Symbolic communication, however, bypasses the thinking mind and goes directly to subconsciousness. In subconsciousness, latent forces are quickened by symbolism, and eventually individuals begin to awaken to the energy world.

Wise teachers in those times knew that anyone awakened enough to understand the symbols and myths would find great meaning in them. The masses, on the other hand, would be able to find meaning at their own level, and thus would not feel threatened by the Teachings.[1] Within mainline Christianity, most priests never learned to interpret the symbols; thus they could not reveal the Wisdom to their parishioners.

In Christian society, those who continued to teach the Wisdom after the fourth century did so through secret

---

[1] See Geoffrey Hodson's *Hidden Wisdom in the Holy Bible,* Vols. I & II, Wheaton, IL: Quest Books, 1993.

schools in order to avoid persecution by the Church. They had a powerful incentive to encapsulate their instruction in symbols that the uninitiated would not be able to decipher. They knew the Teachings would be considered heretical by the Church and by society, which was dominated by the Church. Symbolism masked the Teachings and provided a protective secrecy. Two of the more widely known examples of those secret societies still in existence today are the Masonic and Rosicrucian Orders.

Within the Jewish tradition, Kabbalists have maintained an unbroken line from rabbi (teacher) to student down to the present age, often passing the Teachings from father to son for many generations. Although Kabbalists were often viewed as strange or fanatical, Jews seldom persecuted them, perhaps because the Kabbalists held the Torah as sacred. Nevertheless, since Jews were widely discriminated against, persecuted, and suppressed by Christians, the Kabbalists worked in shadows of secrecy so that their tradition would not be lost.

Was The Western Tradition Of The Teachings Available Only In Secret Schools?

The Wisdom surfaced within Islam in the 8th or 9th century A.D. when seers such as Hasan al-Bari (728 A.D.) began offering a mystical path. Named *Sufis* for the cloth out of which their simple clothes were made, these Islamic seers established Orders and lineages that functioned in both the East and West and that have continued into the present. Mainline Islam has denounced and persecuted the Sufis as an aberrant sect at intervals throughout their history. However, in the 20th Century the Sufis enjoyed a revival that continues to this day.

What Is The Status Of The Wisdom Traditions Today?

Beginning in the last half of the twentieth century, the Eastern and Western streams of Wisdom Teachings began to converge. Several factors have contributed to this relatively new phenomenon. Travel around the globe is easy for both students and teachers. Electronic media make foreign cultures and traditions readily accessible. The rise of democracies in the West has brought about a separation of church and state, making it easier to disseminate the Wisdom openly in the West. And at the end of the nineteenth century, teachers in both traditions began to publish in books what had previously been transmitted only by word of mouth.

An additional factor seems to be the growing number of individuals who are stepping onto the spiritual path. With so many students ready to receive them, teachers of the Wisdom felt a strong urge to make the Teachings available in as many different forms as possible to meet the need. Consequently, you can find your way to the Teachings in local bookstores or on the Internet.

What Have These Wisdom Traditions Taught?

The Wisdom Teachings have always consisted of two complementary aspects: the theoretical and the practical. Both aspects are considered essential to the transmission of the Wisdom.

The theoretical teachings are intended to train the thinking mind by aligning its reasoning processes with the way things actually function in the energy world.

Since most of our thought processes are governed by false impressions, and beliefs based on those impressions, the restructuring of our mental processes takes much time and patience.

The practical teachings actually train us to have our own direct experiences of the energy world and thus to perceive directly the truths being transmitted.

Chapter Three

THE SACRED SCIENCE

What Is The Theoretical Aspect Of The Wisdom?

The Sacred, or Divine, Science is a description of the structure, function, and order of the universe, of humanity, and of the relationship between the two. These Teachings reveal the laws and principles that are fundamental to the universe in which we live. Once these principles are understood, we can begin to learn, in practical terms, how to cooperate with them. The Sacred Science also explains the nature of the forces at work in and through those laws and principles.

The term "science" is used because Wisdom students are always taught not to accept anything on faith alone, but rather to test all presentations of truth through their own experience and to accept them only if they prove valid in the laboratory of Self.

Though terminologies vary from culture to culture and from teacher to teacher, the essence of the truth perceived by seers is amazingly consistent. As seekers and students, however, we must learn to understand what the terms point to, rather than to stumble over words.

What Do The Wisdom Traditions Teach About God?

In all traditions, the Supreme Being is held to be completely unknowable by human consciousness. Though many traditions use a name to refer to this unknowable, inexpressible First Principle that is the source of all we know as the cosmos — a name such as Brahma, Allah, or God — such words are only convenient labels to point to that which is invisible and completely beyond our comprehension.

All Wisdom Traditions tell us that the Original One (that which is unknowable and inexpressible) became two, and the two united to create a third expression. Thus the creating power in the universe is a trinity: Yang, or Father Principle; Yin, or Mother Principle; and the two-in-one (T'ai Chi), or Creating Principle. These three aspects of the Original One are active everywhere in the cosmos, creating, destroying, and preserving the structure and order of all that is so that it can function according to its nature.

This concept of a trinity, of three aspects or expressions of the God Force, can be found in almost all religions. In Hinduism it is especially clear. However, doctrines in Western religions often distort the trinity by leaving out the feminine polarity, as in Judaism, Christianity, and Islam. Belief systems also deny that the destructive force is essential to the creating process by perceiving the Devil as the opponent of God who will be eventually be defeated. And most Christians believe that Jesus of Nazareth is one person in the trinity, thus confusing levels of manifestation. It is, therefore, often difficult to retrain the mind to understand the trinity as it is taught in the Wisdom Traditions if you are a Westerner.

The triune Divine Force is active in an ongoing process of creation, according to the Wisdom. It did not do all its work in six days (even if those days are understood metaphorically) and then rest for the remainder of eternity. Rather, it is an ongoing and active force now, at work in all that is. Neither is this triune Divine Force a fixed "something" that was complete from the beginning of time. Rather, it is emerging in and through the unfolding process in which humanity is participating.

This understanding of the Original One represents a radical difference between the Wisdom Teachings and, for example, Christian theology. Most Christians would find it hard to comprehend the idea that even God does not yet know all that can emerge as the creating process continues. Neither could most Christians imagine that the God Force Itself is emerging, becoming, and growing through the unfolding process that scientists call evolution.

Most Christians are taught that God created the world in six days and then rested. To imagine God as an unfinished project provides a great challenge to most people raised in the Christian church.

What Else Does The Wisdom Teach About God?

We are assured that, although the First Principle is beyond our human understanding, much can be known by inference, because the Original One makes Itself known through every aspect of the cosmic process. The Egyptians taught that one book holds all the secrets of life: the book of nature. Therefore, if we study the world around us, we will come to know the Original One, or God. Initiates of the Wisdom believe that the very scientists who most religious people in the West have long considered secular are revealing the nature of God through their research and experiments.

Most Westerners, with the exception of Native Americans and the Celts, are particularly inept at reading the book of nature in order to learn the inner secrets of life. In the West we have focused on *using* nature rather than communing with it, and we have lost the sense of reverence that would enable us to learn *from* nature rather than seeking to dominate it.

Western scientists are doing their best to reveal nature's secrets. Perhaps they will eventually teach our culture a new regard for the Wisdom that nature manifests. For example, Western scientists are gradually discovering how interwoven all aspects of the life process are, and how interdependent all life forms are. Imagine if we were to learn from those discoveries that we humans are not separate from, or superior to, the natural world around us. That would indeed revolutionize the way we relate to our small planet and utilize its natural resources, to give only one example.

What Is The Structure Of The Universe, According To The Wisdom Teachings?

The Wisdom tells us that out of Its threefold nature the Original One emitted four additional rays of creative energy. The energetic structure of the cosmos reflects those seven creative rays. Thus the numbers three (representing the triune Divine Force), four (representing the additional creative energy rays), and seven (representing the sum of the creative expressions of the Original One) are fundamental to the structure of the universe. The geometric expressions of those numbers, that is, the forms that represent them, are the triangle (3), the square (4), and the pyramid (7, as represented by the square base and the triangles that rise from it). These numbers and forms are found throughout nature on all levels.

In most traditions, the Seven Rays of creative force emanating from the Original One are associated with qualities that reveal the essence, or nature, of the One. Attributes commonly attributed to the Seven Rays are Will, Activity (that is, motion, vibration, and thus, consciousness), Love (or Wisdom), Science (or Knowledge), Devotion, Harmony, and Ceremony (or Order).

In addition, the Wisdom tells us that there are four "worlds" that constitute the basic structure of the cosmos. We might call them fields of energy, or vast wavebands of energy. Those worlds are given various names according to the different traditions. The first is the World of Divine Emanation (called Atziluth by the Kabbalists). The emanations do not yet have any form. They are rays of Light substance that cause energy to begin to take form. This first world is sometimes called the Causal World, or the world of divine activity.

Though we usually think of "substance" as physical, the Wisdom Teachings view the entire creating process as dealing with substance in varying degrees of fineness or denseness. In other words, the wave frequencies of the energy world go from the extremely rapid movement of imperceptibly short waves in the first world to the slow, large waves of the fourth world that are perceptible to our five human senses. Thus what is called the Light substance of the first world is not light as we perceive it in the fourth world, measured in light years. Rather it is something so brilliant and rapid that it would blind our physical eyes. The Kabbalists regard it as "darkness on the face of the deep," a light too brilliant to be "seen." The first world might also, therefore, be called the Light Mother, because it is out of the womb of these emanations that the cosmos is birthed.

The second is the world of Creation (called Briah by the Kabbalists). In this world patterns begin to emerge in Mind substance. Consequently, it is often called the World of Mind, or the Mind of God. This is beyond our direct experience as humans and is not to be confused with our thinking mind and the ordinary consciousness in which we function. We might also term this the World Mother, since out of this Mind substance is born the world of form.

The patterns in Mind substance are called archetypes. They are the fundamental patterns from which all forms are derived. The archetypes are not "things." Plato called this the Realm of Ideas, though these ideas should not be thought of as mental. They are, rather, lines of force which have not yet been clothed with qualities and characteristics that can be identified as forms.

The third is the world of Formation (called Yetzirah by the Kabbalists). Here forms begin to take on astral substance, which is subtler than material substance but human consciousness is able to perceive it. This third realm is often called the Astral World; it encompasses all that belongs to our human psyches.

Finally, there is the World of Matter (called Assiah by the Kabbalists). This is the world of nature as we know it, and of human existence. It is the realm that we call physical and is composed of material substance, which is energy moving at very slow vibrational rates.

These four worlds are, according to the Wisdom Teachings, fundamental to the structure of the universe.

In each world there are Beings who correspond to the qualities of the Seven Rays. They are, in effect, emissaries of the Original One, giving expression to the essence of the Divine in these different phases of the ongoing creating process. In the Realm of Emanation, the Beings are called gods, or Attributes of God, such as Kingship, Wisdom, Understanding, Mercy, Justice, Beauty, Power, Glory, Creativity, and Presence. In the Creational World the Beings are called Choirs of Angels, and include Seraphim, Cherubim, Thrones, Dominions, Virtues, Powers, Principalities, Archangels, and Angels. In the Realm of Formation, the Beings are the Sun and Moon, the five planets visible to the naked eye, the Earth, the sphere of the fixed stars, and "the Primum Mobile, the clear crystal sphere which keeps everything going." We are not accustomed to think of stars and planets, the sun and the moon, as emanating energy that expresses the Original One, but the Wisdom Teachings have always done so. (Knight 52) Finally, the Beings in the Material World are called Elementals, the creative forces behind nature. They include Nature Spirits, Angelic Overlords, Devas, and Elemental Kings, among others.

It is easy to see that this theoretical presentation of the Divine Science is not of much use to us if it remains theoretical. We are told, for example, that human beings can learn to communicate and cooperate with these emissaries of the Divine. Yet until we develop our subtle senses, as occurs during the process of awakening described in Part Two below, such communication seems quite out of reach and impossible. That is why no instruction in the Wisdom is complete unless it includes both the theoretical and the practical.

What Are The Universal Laws and Principles Taught In The Wisdom Tradition?

The laws and principles at work in the cosmos are given different expression in different traditions. In the West perhaps the most familiar formulation of the laws is attributed to Hermes Trismegistus.[2] The broad outline provided here is meant to whet your appetite so that you will pursue a deeper grasp of these laws through extensive study and through your practical application and experience.

As presented in *Kybalion*,[3] the Hermetic Principles are:

1. The Principle of Mentalism: The substantial reality, which brought into being everything that we can register with our physical senses, is spirit or Mind (as in the second world of creation mentioned above). It is, to the human being, unknowable and indefinable, but it is *analogous* to what we know in our human experience as inspiration or intuitive insight.

2. The Principle of Correspondences: Often stated, "As above, so below; as below, so above." There is always a correspondence between the laws and phenomena of the various levels of being and life. Therefore, we can know something of the Unknowable by studying what we experience as humans and using our reason to ex-

---

[2] The ancient Egyptians regarded Hermes as the embodiment of the Universal Mind. "Trismegistus" means "the thrice greatest," the greatest of all philosophers, the greatest of all priests, and the greatest of all kings. See Manly P. Hall, *the Secret Teachings of All Ages,* Los Angeles: The Philosophical Research Society, 1977, page XXXVII.

[3] *The Kybalion* by Three Initiates, Chicago, IL: The Yogi Publication Society, Masonic Temple, 1936.

trapolate what that tells us about both lower and higher levels.[4]

3. The Principle of Vibration: Everything is in motion; nothing rests and everything moves and vibrates. In other words, we live in an energy world. This principle is not surprising to us now that our physicists describe the fundamental nature of our universe as vibrating atoms of energy.

4. The Principle of Polarity: Everything has its pair of opposites. We live in a universe of duality in which "'opposites' are really only the two extremes of the same thing, with many varying degrees between them." (*Kybalion* 32)[5]

5. The Principle of Rhythm: Everything in our universe moves in rhythmic cycles of out and in, back and forth, up and down. These pendulum swings are predictable on all levels, even in the mental states of human beings.

6. The Principle of Cause and Effect: Often known as the Law of Karma. Everything happens according to law or, as the popular new age expression puts it, there are no accidents. Learning how to work with this law is one of the keys to mastery of our human expression and to liberation from suffering.

7. The Principle of Gender: The word "gender" means "that which engenders (creates)" and thus refers to the principle of yin and yang that is at work on all levels of the cosmos. Whenever anything is brought into be-

---

[4] The author's book *Life As A Waking Dream*, New York: Riverhead Books, 1997, uses the Principle of Correspondences to probe the meaning of personal life experiences.

[5] In Arleen Lorrance's novel *The Two*, Scottsdale, AZ: Teleos Imprint, 2003, the main characters grapple with the Principle of Polarity, seeking to understand it in practical terms.

ing, whether through generation (the reproductive processes), regeneration (the transformation of energies by changes in consciousness), or creation (bringing new forms into being), yin and yang unite to bring it about. Yin and yang are present within every thing and every person.

This brief summary statement of the Hermetic Principles cannot do justice to the depth of the Teachings they represent. To live according to these laws takes years of study and integration, but at least we have taken the essential first step by becoming aware that they exist.

What Does The Wisdom Tradition Teach About Humanity?

The Wisdom Teachings hold that human beings are a microcosmic image of the Original One, the macrocosm. The inner and invisible "real Self" of the human being, like the essence of the invisible First Principle of the cosmos, comprises three principal functions: Will, Consciousness, and Unconditional Love (or Wisdom). This invisible, triune "real Self" is often referred to as "God Within," the Higher Triad, or the Higher Self.

In fact, the Wisdom Teachings hold that humans are not different in *nature* from the triune Divine Force, but only in the degree to which the divine powers are made manifest. This is a different understanding of the nature of humans from the traditional Christian doctrine that humans are born in sin and thus are separated from God. The Wisdom teaches that the divine spark within each human, which is a manifestation of our oneness with God, works to bring forth those intrinsic powers to greater and greater degrees. In Part Two below I describe the process of awakening during which the divine powers begin to unfold within the individual.

As a reflection of the First Principle described above under the Sacred Science, the triune real Self of the individual human expresses through a Lower Quaternary, known as the mental, emotional, etheric, and physical bodies. These bodies express the universal attributes of knowledge (or science), devotion, harmony, and order (or ceremony) first emanated by the triune Divine Force.

If Humans Are Made In The Image Of God, Why Are We Not Able To Manifest Our Divinity?

The Wisdom Traditions teach that there is no separation between the Original One and humankind. We are one in nature and indivisible throughout all time (Hodson 36-39). Any apparent separation (or "sin," as the Bible calls it) is only in the consciousness of the human being, and is inculcated by the culture in which the human lives. In addition, when we identify with one or more of the four vehicles through which the real Self expresses, we believe ourselves to *be* that vehicle. We then feel separate from the All. Through the process of awakening described in Part Two below, the individual comes to know self as the Higher Triad (the real Self), which is spirit or Mind, and all sense of separation disappears.

The Higher Triad and the Lower Quaternary of the human being are infused by and radiate out the Seven Rays of the Original One through the seven energy centers that are active in the developing autonomous field of human beings. Thus, humans, through a study of their own microcosmic sevenfold nature can come to know the macrocosmic, divine nature. As below so above.

If Humans Are Created In The Image Of The Original One, Does This Mean We Are Special And Different From The Rest Of Creation?

The Wisdom teaches us that human beings are an integral part of Nature, not separate from it. There are two phases in the creating process: infolding and unfolding. In the infolding process, the yang force and the yin substance work together as a united creative force to bring the essence of the Original One into form. From the emergence of the first atom until the development of the human being, forms increase in complexity and diversity until a vehicle for self-consciousness is formed. The second half of the creating process, which begins with the human being, takes place in consciousness. Individuals unfold in their own consciousness a knowledge of Self as All that Is. This unfolding process begins with the process of awakening described in Part Two below.

This teaching is different from the Biblical Creation story as it is usually understood, which makes it seem that humans were created by a special act of God and that God intended for humans to "rule" the rest of Nature. The Wisdom Teachings, by contrast, tell us that humans emerged out of the preceding millennial creating process, not by the special act of a separate creator. Moreover, humans were not created to "rule" the rest of Nature, but rather to live in cooperation and harmony with it. Those of us brought up on the Biblical Creation story are so conditioned to think and believe that humans are creations separate from God and Nature that it is difficult to grasp, on initial exposure, how different this teaching actually is.

It would be fair to say that human beings play a special role in the ongoing creating process as they awaken in consciousness, but not because they were made by a special act of creation. Rather, humans emerge out of and are an integral part of the creating process.

If Humans Were Not Born In Sin, Then Why Do We Experience Ourselves As Separate From God?

According to the Wisdom, human beings live in what is often called "maya" or "illusion." This simply means that in our ordinary consciousness we do not register, touch, or become conscious of the energy world as it really is. When the four vehicles that constitute the Lower Quaternary are sufficiently developed, humans begin to feel the urge to know something more. That urge eventually awakens the real Self. Maya[6] falls away as the human learns to live in the energy world, even if the culture in which he or she lives does not acknowledge the validity of this knew mode of perception. Part Two below describes this process of awakening.

What Is The Purpose Of Human Life?

When addressing the purpose of human life, the Wisdom Teachings speak of the Great Work to which individuals must devote themselves. Although we humans are already in union with the Original One by nature, in

---

[6] The author developed a method for working with the maya, called Life As A Waking Dream, to make it possible for individuals to profit from their life experiences rather than to let them go to waste. See Pike, *Life As A Waking Dream*.

our consciousness of Self we need to grow and evolve. This book provides an overview of that Great Work.

Geoffrey Hodson puts it this way:

> *The purpose of human life is spiritual, intellectual, cultural, and physical evolution. This is a dual process, consisting on the one hand of the gradual unfoldment from latency to full potency of one's threefold spiritual attributes, and on the other, of the evolution of the four material vehicles to a condition in which they perfectly make manifest the developed powers of the human spirit. Life in a physical body is essential to this attainment. ... The resultant human individuality in its four vehicles is strengthened by the winds of adversity, purified and refined by the rain of sorrow, beautified and expanded by the sunshine of happiness and love, and ultimately reaches the fully flowered state. ... All experience is valuable; nothing is wasted. (Hodson 40-41).*

Implicit in this quotation from Hodson is the principle of rhythm, namely, that life is cyclical, not linear. Just as in nature there is a cycle from year to year of rebirth in the spring, flowering in the summer, harvest in the autumn, and dormancy in the winter, so human evolution proceeds in a rhythmic fashion. The human cycle begins with birth into a new physical vehicle, which has the capacity to move, and thus to express the individual's will. Three additional vehicles are then developed. The etheric body is composed of a substance less dense than the physical. It is affected by feelings and thoughts and passes those imprints on to the physical. The emotional body develops within astral substance and has the capacity to register the effect of living under the influence of the law of polarity. That awareness takes the form of feelings. The mental body is the last to develop. Also composed of astral substance, the mental body has the capacity to think and its expressions take the form of thoughts. The etheric, emotional, and mental bodies are what we refer to as the psyche, or soul, of the human being.

In the summertime of the human cycle, when all four bodies are mature (usually by or before the individual is 30 years old), the flower that is put forth is the Higher Triad (the spirit). In the fall, the human harvests (1) qualities of being, such as kindness and patience, (2) faculties of consciousness, such as the ability to hear the inner voice and to reason according to the laws and principles mentioned above, and (3) life skills, such as confidence in expressing oneself (whether in words or in action) and the ability to form intimate relationships. These are the "treasures laid up in heaven" of which Jesus spoke.

In the winter of the human cycle, the four vehicles wither and die, the physical first, and then the other three. The developing consciousness of the Higher Triad lies dormant until the next birth. Latent within it are the qualities, faculties, and life skills harvested at the end of the previous lifetime. During this wintertime, between lifetimes, we absorb and integrate what we learned and developed in the cycle just ended. But according to the Wisdom Teachings, we are not able to unfold further until we once again put forth four vehicles of experience and expression.

A new body and psyche are formed in the spring of a new cycle. In the new psyche, the attributes previously developed will seem to be natural to the developing child. People will observe, "That's just the way she is." The faculties of consciousness developed in the previous cycle will make themselves known as intuitive abilities, and the life skills will be viewed as talents. In other words, what has been developed in previous cycles of growth (previous lifetimes) constitutes the individual differences between children born of the same parents and within the same community.

Those who believe that it is the personality that reincarnates misunderstand this teaching. In fact, the personality, which is usually identified by the qualities and temperament the individual expresses, is the superficial manifestation of the psyche. The personality, and the psyche it represents, also dies in what is called the "second death" in the New Testament. Therefore, when those who are identified with their personalities, believing they *are* their feelings and thoughts and the patterns of behavior they have developed, say "I" lived before, they are mistaken. The seed that lies hidden in the energy world until it is born again is the real Self (the Spirit). Only after the process of awakening is complete can one say, "*I* have lived before," for then the individual is identified with the real Self that has emerged in the course of many cycles of living.

During the process of awakening, individuals sometimes experience past life recalls. These are glimpses of other incarnations of the real Self sometimes remembered in vivid imagery. Or we might recognize another real Self (Spirit) when we are introduced to the personality it is wearing in this lifetime. Or, we might remember a place even though we have not visited it before in this lifetime. Or, we may remember a lesson hard learned in another lifetime. Generally speaking, these glimpses come only when they are relevant to the current process of learning and unfolding that is occurring for and in us. Sometimes they represent a temptation to divert our energies into an expression that is not relevant to this lifetime. In those cases, we need to acknowledge the recall, ask ourselves what we learned from that lifetime, and move on from it. Sometimes the recalls are related to current growing edges, and they help us to integrate what we are learning into our unfolding consciousness.

What Laws And Principles Apply To The Human?

There are universal laws and forces at work in the human being just as there are in the cosmos. In order to become co-creators with the Original One during the unfolding process, we must learn to understand how our own bodies and psyches function so that we can consciously direct those processes that are now automatic.

Through a study of the Wisdom we learn:

1. The psyche, which comprises our feeling and thinking functions, is made of astral substance and functions by reflection and suggestion. In infancy, we learn how to function in the world by watching and listening to those around us. Throughout our lives, we change the content of the psyche only by exposing ourselves to new influences. To claim our psyches as our own, we must choose what to reflect and what new patterns to inculcate through repetition.

2. We are integrated in group energy fields that strongly influence the formation of our psyches. The largest field we might simply label "humanity." It holds the fundamental pattern for the form and function of our bodies and psyches. Then within that largest field there are fields within fields within fields. For example, there are racial and ethnic group fields that imprint us with certain qualities and characteristics. Within those groups are national identity group fields, religious identity group fields, personal family group fields, peer group fields, professional fields, and other special interest group fields. Each of these fields influences the formation of our private worlds of values, opinions, beliefs, and world views, as well as the way we actually function in the world around us. To free ourselves from the unconscious influence of these group fields, we must each build an autonomous field by coming to know the real Self.

3. We are motivated by forces moving through the energy world in which we are integrated. The way we function in the energy world and the way we *think* we function are two different things. No matter what values and convictions we hold, we are motivated by the frequencies we register. We register the frequencies for which we have an affinity, and we have affinities for those frequencies that carry qualities similar to those that are active in our own psyches. Therefore, to change our urges and motivations, we must first learn to discriminate between the private world of our ordinary awareness and the functional energy world. Then we must learn to transmute the qualities in our psyches so that our affinities will, in turn, change. Learning such discrimination and transmutation is a major part of the process of awakening described below.

4. The real Self (or Higher Triad) determines the qualities that are active in the psyche and body. Once we become conscious of the real Self (or Higher Triad), we can cleanse body and psyche so that they reflect without distortion the pattern held in the real Self. At that point, the real Self becomes determinative regarding the qualities that are active in the psyche and body. We will find new group fields within which to function and we will orient ourselves to a higher influence than humanity: the Christos, or the Noetic Mind. We will emerge as a new order of being, no longer merely human, and function in a higher state of consciousness. We will have completed the process of awakening and will continue the unfolding process as conscious co-creators with the Original One.

What Are "The Secrets" Of Initiation?

The secrets of initiation are certain spiritual practices that speed up the unfolding process so that we can prove (or disprove) *through our own experience* the truths taught in the Sacred Science. Until this past century, living teachers guided all but a few rare individuals through the initiatory process, and they passed on these secrets. Teachers took responsibility for their students' well being and supervised their various spiritual disciplines and practices to make sure they advanced in an integrated and balanced way. In our time, however, growing numbers of aspirants have to find their own way, without living teachers and often without even finding groups with whom to share.

Although it is possible to find our way without a living teacher, it is helpful to have some guidelines to go by. It is my hope that the description of the process of awakening that follows will serve that purpose.

PART TWO

THE PRACTICAL

Chapter Four

THE PROCESS OF AWAKENING

We are drawn to the Wisdom Teachings because we have begun to awaken to our true nature, which is consciousness. In all traditions we are urged to test the validity of the theoretical teachings in our everyday lives. As we do that, we gain deeper insight into our human nature, and through that self-knowledge we grow in our understanding of the nature of the universe and of the indefinable Power behind it. The *process* of awakening is the practical side of the Wisdom Teachings.

There are two principles from the Wisdom Teachings that guide us as we describe the process of awakening. One is the principle that human beings are a part of Nature, that we emerged out of the same creating process as did rocks, plants and animals. Therefore, to study our human unfolding we utilize the same techniques of observation, examination, and reason as we would in the study of any other aspect of nature.

The other is the Hermetic principle of correspondence: as above, so below, as below, so above; as within, so without, as without, so within. In other words, we look for correspondences between humans and minerals, plants, and animals. One of the symbols used for many years to represent the potential that lies within us is the seed. The seed comes to us from plant life. Looking at the seed as a metaphor for our own process of growth helps us to gain a new perspective.

We know, for example, that a seed holds the pattern of the plant that will emerge from it. By analogy we can reason that for us, as human beings, there must be something *like* a seed to guide our growth and development. On the physical level we regard the fertilized egg as that kind of seed, because we know that it holds the genes that determine the characteristics of our physical body. But we are not only our bodies. From very early in our development, even when we are still babies, we also have personalities. Do the genes carry the seeds of the personality? Not that scientists have been able to trace. Then what does?

The Wisdom teaches us that the personality is formed of astral substance, not physical matter. This means that the seed of the personality will not be available for study with our physical senses. We will have to apply our reason based on higher principles to understand the development of the personality/psyche/soul.[1] And we will need to work with the law of correspondences even more extensively to understand the seed of the real Self, or spirit.

The human seed unfolds on three different levels, body (both physical and etheric), soul, and spirit, something like the development of a plant, with its roots, stem, and leaves. In the process of awakening, we come to know ourselves at each of the three levels.

---

[1] I use the term "soul" as synonymous with the term "psyche" (the Greek term for soul). I think of the personality as a kind of mask (the Greek word "persona" means mask) that makes the psyche visible through patterns of behavior and identifiable characteristics. Not all people use these terms in this way, as is the case in the quotation at the beginning of the next chapter where "soul" is used to represent what I would call the "autonomous field" or the "spirit."

Will The Development Of Every Human Seed Be Identical?

Before scientists could develop a generalized description of plant life, they observed a large variety of plants. Based on extensive observation over many years, generalizations about common patterns were abstracted and the peculiarities of given species noted. We know, for example, that flowering plants follow the general pattern of putting forth first a flower, then fruit, and finally the seed of new beginning. According to the given species, however, the actual form of the flower, fruit and seed changes dramatically. If we did not know the overall pattern, we might not recognize that the cone of a pine tree serves the same function as an apple, or that the featherlike parachute that carries a dandelion seed on the wind shares the task of dissemination with a bird that eats a cherry and drops the seed in its feces. The overall pattern is that the fruit holds the new seed within itself and releases it into the world as the fruit falls away. Knowing the overall pattern helps us to identify the stages of development within a given species of plant. Comparing one unique expression (a cone) with another (an apple) without an overview might elucidate nothing.

The same is true of human beings. Only those who have observed a sufficient number of human beings during the awakening process can offer a generalized description of the *pattern* of unfolding. The phases, looked at in the lives of individuals, might take on such different forms and aspects that we might not see any similarity if comparing one person's experience directly to another. Seers through the ages, however, have given us the gift of an overview. The overview makes it possible to see individual experiences of the unfolding process as examples of the larger pattern that governs humanity. By learning to identify the pattern, we gain understanding and a sense of orientation.

Is This Overall Pattern Of Unfolding An Indication Of The Right Way To Do The Process Of Awakening?

It is easy to see why it is not helpful for a given species of plant to try to prescribe for others how they should do the generative process. Fruit trees, for example, might decide there is only one unselfish way to reproduce, and that is to couch one's seed in an edible fruit that will nourish other creatures higher on the evolutionary scale before the next cycle is begun by the seed. They might feel superior to, or even condemn, milk pods, dandelions, and other plants for their profligate wastefulness, since they bear thousands of seeds, none of which is wrapped in edible substance, and simply scatter them on the wind.

Applying this nature analogy, we can also see why it is not helpful for people to tell others *how they ought to unfold*, that is, what form their expressions of the process of awakening should take. For example, rules and formulas are often offered for how to pray, how to express one's love for God in worship or in service, how to live one's life in a godly fashion, and what intellectual formulas (beliefs) to adopt. Variations from the prescribed norm are sometimes condemned as heretical, immoral, misguided, and/or sinful. Such judgments focus on specific expressions and actions as right or wrong. Universal patterns that embrace all religious and non-religious expressions of the natural order process of unfolding are <u>de</u>scriptive rather than <u>pre</u>scriptive. They describe what *does* happen rather than what *should*.

The Wisdom Teachings encourage us to take nothing from another *on faith alone*. We are urged to try out particular approaches described by others to see if we can verify them in our own experience. What we come to *know* through our own experience does not need to be formulated as a belief, nor can it be taken away from us by persuasions presented by others.

By this 21st Century many of us have already moved beyond belief to personal knowing. We have developed a profound trust in the natural order process to which we belong. This is faith of a different order. It is not faith in someone else's word. It is faith in the pattern encoded in our own nature, guiding our development, motivating us from within. It is faith in the real Self as part of the Whole, integral to the universe that is our home.

Those who are motivated to know their place in the Whole have begun to awaken.

How Do We Awaken?

Each day each of us wakes from sleep. The manner of waking from sleep is different for different persons, and different for each of us from time to time.

We can wake suddenly when something startles us, causing us to return to our ordinary, objective consciousness[2] so quickly that we are disoriented. Millennia-old instinctual patterns evolved during the animal phase of

---

[2] Objective consciousness is the norm for human beings. In that state we perceive ourselves to be living in an objective-to-self world populated by things and objects separate from self. We see ourselves as objects among other objects, with space separating us from each and every other.

development surface quickly. Our hearts pound to circulate energy so we can meet any situation that arises. Adrenalin rushes through our systems, preparing us for "fight or flight." Our senses strain to discover what woke us. Often it takes several moments to recall where we are and sometimes even who we are. After the initial emergency reaction, our human reason takes over and we move into our normal state of functioning in objective awareness.

Such sudden awakenings also occur in other areas of functioning. We might suddenly awaken, for example, from objective consciousness to psychic[3], or astral, awareness. This reality is as different from our ordinary state as being awake is from being physically asleep. To awaken to psychic perception suddenly, with no preparation, can startle the human data-processing system and cause confusion or imbalance. We might, for example, begin to hear voices, see entities that are not in physical bodies, appear to leave our bodies in what is called astral travel, see future events before they happen, or have images of past lives overlay what is transpiring in the present.

Such a sudden awakening might be precipitated by energy events such as the use of drugs, physical injury to the coccyx, severe emotional or psychological trauma, intense meditation or breath work, or sustained participation in a highly charged group field. Or sometimes the

---

[3] Psychic consciousness perceives forms in the astral world that do not appear to be "solid" like material objects, but do appear to be discrete, that is, separate and distinct from one another. These forms can pass through material objects and each other without losing their shape and they are not bound by the parameters of time and space that govern the physical world. Still, they seem to be separate from each other as physical objects seem to be.

seed within self is simply growing according to its natural rhythm, even though the personality is unprepared for the experiences that accompany that growth.

The individual awakened suddenly to psychic awareness usually responds by being profoundly disoriented and often experiences great fear. I knew a young man whom we shall call Ron whose psychic perception opened when he was a freshman in college. He began to see events before they happened, and to know things that he had never been told. Ron was, at the time, dating a young lady who was active in a fundamentalist Christian organization and he used to attend meetings with her. Suddenly he found himself at the center of a storm of controversy. He was told that his new "powers" were "of the devil" and that his soul was in jeopardy. Since Ron did not have any other way to understand what was transpiring, he became full of fear and foreboding. He was afraid that, by foreseeing them, he was somehow *causing* those events to happen.

It was not very long until Ron began to have a nervous breakdown because of his distress over his experiences. Medical doctors did not know what to do for him. They put him in a psychiatric hospital and medicated him heavily to dull his newly awakened sensitivities. Ron remained "mentally ill" for nearly twenty years. With the unconditional love and support of his family, he was finally able to build his self-confidence enough to function normally (namely, in the objective state of consciousness). Eventually he returned to college and took up where he left off, but without his psychic faculties.

Ron is an example of someone without an overview. He had no understanding of what was happening when he suddenly awakened into a new state of awareness. He thought he was "going crazy," and his friends and the medical community confirmed his suspicions. If he had understood the process of awakening, he could have turned for guidance to someone who recognized that he had opened a new faculty of perception.

Is There Any Other Way To Respond To An Abrupt Awakening?

When we wake suddenly from physical sleep, animal instincts handle the first moments of the emergency. However, when we awaken abruptly from objective consciousness into higher states of consciousness, we can only rely on understanding and training gained from others who have gone through the process before us. Sometimes that training occurs within the same lifetime as the awakening. In other cases, training was received in past lives and we are able to rely on intuition to get through a sudden awakening. However, if we have not been prepared on the personality level in this lifetime to integrate the new consciousness and we do not soon get help, some disorientation may remain, perhaps for the rest of a lifetime. Such persons often become dysfunctional. They are unable to orient themselves in time and space and they are unclear as to who they really are. They are no longer "asleep," but neither have they developed the ability to function well in their awakened states of consciousness. Many spend time in psychiatric institutions.

I knew a man named Ray who was startled into an awakened state when he was sent out as a pilot on a bombing mission during the Korean War. After he took off from his home base, he realized that he could not drop bombs on people. It went against his inner nature. He thought perhaps he could fly his plane off the planet, but when that did not work, he returned to base, his mission unfulfilled.

When Ray explained to his superiors why he had returned to base, he was quickly sent home for psychiatric care. He tried to explain that he could see and communicate with entities others thought were dead, that he had guides who gave him instruction in nonobjective realms, that he was not allowed to take the life of any sentient being, and so forth. The doctors listened to him and finally "certified" him as insane. He lived the rest of his life in and out of psychiatric facilities, doing his best to function in ordinary society with the help of medication that dulled his "abnormal" sensitivities, but never quite managing. He knew he was not insane, but he also knew that society viewed him that way. The few who understood his altered states of consciousness were not enough to help him stabilize his awakening.

Still another man I knew, whom we shall call Harold, had his psychic faculties open suddenly. He began to see and hear entities in the psychic realm who did not have physical bodies. He told his wife about his experiences, and she had him committed to a mental hospital. Harold quickly learned that he would never get out unless he stopped reporting his experiences. Once he was released from the hospital he talked of his experiences only when he knew the one to whom he spoke would understand.

Harold expressed his relief when he learned that I understood his experiences. He talked at length about these friends in the astral realm who met him at the bus stop and walked home with him, or who visited him in the evenings, etc. He could tell the difference between these people and people who had physical bodies, so he did not confuse the two realms. This enabled him to function in both worlds and maintain his mental balance. He had established an overview through the exercise of his own reason, and that helped him to function normally as far as most people knew. Yet he did not feel completely isolated because he was able to find his way to others who understood the astral realm.

A wider general understanding in society of the process of awakening would help to prevent incidents of awakening from going awry. There are psychiatrists, such as Lee Sannella and Stanislav Grof,[4] who have recognized the need for intervention in such instances. Grof, with his wife Christina, established a Spiritual Emergence Network to help those who have sudden awakenings and are not prepared to integrate them into their objective consciousness.

Do All People Who Awaken Experience Such Frightening Disorientation?

Again, analogy helps us to see other possibilities. There is another kind of sudden waking from an ordinary night's sleep. It is natural, gentle, and easy. One moment, it would seem, we are sound asleep. In the next moment we open our eyes, fully alert. Nothing has jarred us. We are not conscious of a transition. We do not struggle to wake nor do we spend time in a kind of twilight zone. We simply wake up, spontaneously.

There are persons who experience such spontane-

---

[4] Lee Sannella, M.D. wrote *Kundalini: Psychosis or Transcendence?* San Francisco: H. S. Dakin Company, 1977. Stanley Grof, M. D. is the author of many books. With his wife Christina he edited the book *Spiritual Emergency: When Personal Transformation Becomes a Crisis* (New Consciousness Reader), New York: Tarcher/Putnam, 1989, and founded the Spiritual Emergence Network.

ous awakenings to other states of consciousness. With no apparent effort made, with no struggle and no transition, they simply "awaken." One moment they are functioning in the ordinary human state of objective consciousness. In the next moment they are awake to, alive in, and conscious of their integration in a larger Whole. They begin to participate consciously in the vast realm of reality that is beyond the perception of the physical senses.

Such persons do not experience disorientation. There is a continuity of the sense of "I." Everything is suddenly new and different for them, but they move into their new state of consciousness with confidence and ease, making whatever changes are needed to bring their personal lives into alignment with their new and broader awareness. For such persons there is no trauma. Rather, there is a profound knowing that they are at home in themselves and in their world. They operate out of a deep trust that they will find their way into the new that awaits them.

An outstanding example of this kind of sudden awakening is the great Indian saint Ramana Maharshi.[5] Paul Brunton recounts that Ramana was living an ordinary childhood in Northern India when one day, at age 17, he was besieged by a sudden fear of death. Obsessed with the notion that he was about to die, he stretched out on the floor in his bedroom. He stiffened his limbs like the rigidity of a corpse, closed his eyes and mouth, and held his breath.

> *'Well, then,' said I to myself, 'this body is dead. It will be carried stiff to the burning ground and then reduced to*

---

[5] Ramana Maharshi, an Indian saint, was born in 1879 and died in 1950.

> ashes. But with the death of the body, am I dead? Is the body I? This body is now silent and stiff. But I continue to feel the full force of my self apart from its condition.'
>
> Those are the words which Maharishee [which means Great Sage or Seer] used in describing the weird experience through which he passed. What happened next is difficult to understand though easy to describe. He seemed to fall into a profound conscious trance wherein he became merged into the very source of selfhood, the very essence of being. He understood quite clearly that the body was a thing apart and that the I remained untouched by death. The true self was very real, but it was so deep down in man's nature that hitherto he had ignored it. (Brunton 283)

When Ramana awakened from his trance-like state, Brunton reports, he was centered in the sublime consciousness of the true Self. He was fully enlightened, enjoying an inward serenity and a spiritual strength that never left him. The fear of death completely left him. Not long thereafter, he left his school and studies, his friends, and his family to live the life of a hermit in a cave where he could spend his days and nights immersed in profound states of meditation. (Brunton 282-287) He made a seamless transition from unawakened to fully awakened in a matter of a few hours.

What If Neither Of These Extreme Awakenings Occurs?

Most often, to continue with our analogy, we wake in a manner that is somewhere between deep sleep and the sudden and the spontaneous ways described above.

Often there is a period of half-sleep. We are no longer fully asleep, but neither are we fully alert. Sometimes we struggle to pull ourselves out of sleep, and the process seems effortful. We have difficulty waking up. Other times we are waking up, but we do not want to. We want to go back to sleep, to rest awhile longer. Other times, we are conscious that we are waking up and we observe the process, taking note of dreams, being aware of the environment to which we are waking, sensing our bodies, recalling the day past and looking forward to the day to come. We gather a sense of self and of our space/time so that when we are ready, we can step forth into the new day with a feeling of continuity — a throughline from the past, for the present, and into the future.

During this particular time period in our human history, many persons are undergoing this kind of gradual awakening to higher states of consciousness. Some are struggling to awaken. They feel the dragback into objective consciousness and are struggling against it. Their awakening is effortful but eagerly pursued.

I can think of many examples among people in my acquaintance. Some are dealing with physical problems, being overweight, addicted to alcohol or drugs, or suffering with a disease. What sets them apart from others who are not awakening is that these individuals are asking, "Why me? What did I do to bring this condition on? Why can't I simply let go of it? What can I do to heal myself?" The more earnestly they ask questions such as these, the more they stir within their waking dreams.[6]

Others I know are in very difficult relationships or jobs and are suffering emotionally and mentally. These

---

[6] See *Life As A Waking Dream*, by Diane Kennedy Pike, New York: Riverhead Books, 1997.

persons are also asking, "How did I get myself into this? How can I get myself out? Does this mean I am unworthy or just too dumb to exercise good judgment when entering a relationship or taking a job?" They begin to struggle to awaken when they ask, "What can I do to change this situation? What am I learning here?"

Perhaps in these examples you can see that situations and conditions in these people's lives are prodding them to awaken, in much the same way as nightmares often cause us to wake ourselves in the middle of the night. In spite of how painful these situations are, however, it is often difficult to awaken from them. Patterned responses to their life circumstances drag them back into unconsciousness. It is a struggle to identify with the real Self and to perceive the circumstances of their daily lives as dreams from which they can awaken.

What Other Responses Are There To The Urge To Awaken?

Others would just as soon go on sleeping. They are content in their normal human state and have no particular desire to change. Yet they feel a movement from within. No matter how they try to settle back, remain as they were, or stop the process, they are awakening.

I remember a young woman whom we shall call Lori who was riding the wave of the technological boom in the 1990's. She had invented a software program that was going to revolutionize the way businesses handle their finances. Lori was determined to make a fortune and retire early so she could live out her deepest desires. At about the midpoint of her business plan, Lori began to feel restless. In her heart she longed for something more. She tried to convince herself to stay with her business plan until she made her fortune. The restlessness grew.

Lori was at the beginning of an opening of her heart center. She could feel it, but the timing didn't fit her plan. She tried to slow it down. She bargained with it. She said, "I'll use my vacation time to go to India." The restlessness eased off. When the time came for her vacation, Lori could hardly wait to leave for India. During her two weeks there, her heart opened wide. She knew she had to do something more meaningful than to make a fortune.

Lori tried hard to convince herself that she could wait. She reasoned, what would it hurt to delay for another five years? But her heart would not be stilled. She ended up selling her software for a modest price just to get out of the business. She is now happily working with orphaned children in New York City, fulfilling her heart's desire rather than her business plan. She couldn't delay the awakening even though she tried.

Still others neither resist their awakening nor struggle to make it happen, but they are experiencing the transformation. They observe the process that is occurring, sometimes fascinated by it, other times confused. Many are conscious of psychic experiences (the dreamstates of objective consciousness). Others glimpse higher frequencies, taste bliss, and know peace for brief periods. Nearly all seek to trace the continuity between who they have been and who they are becoming.

Often these people join study groups, read a lot, and take up certain spiritual practices. But what is most important is that they simply go on living their lives. Nothing much changes in their outer life, but every day they are as aware of inner changes as they are of the rising sun. They don't make a big deal of their inner changes, but they do observe them and honor them, integrating them with how they live each day.

Anyone who is experiencing an awakening, whether sudden, spontaneous, effortful, easy, or gentle, will benefit greatly from an overview of the process of awakening. It is my hope that with this description in hand, you will be able to identify where you are in the process when you awaken to new states of consciousness. Then you will be able to reorient yourself so that you can continue to function effectively in your current time/space with enhanced faculties of awareness.

Who Is Asleep And Who Awakens?

To continue with the analogy used above, the same self who goes to sleep at night is the one who wakes up in the morning. Yet while we are unconscious – that is, while the body is asleep – it *seems* the self no longer exists. *We are usually not aware of being the self while we are asleep.* We are not functioning in objective awareness during a dream and thus self-consciousness is not available to us. When we wake from sleep, we recover, or reclaim, our self-consciousness.

Similarly, there is only one Self who is conscious of Self. Yet to the real Self, the objective state of consciousness (our ordinary human mode of functioning) is like a dream within deep sleep, or unconsciousness. While we function in our human self-consciousness *we are not aware of being the real Self.* It seems to most humans that the real Self does not exist, or cannot be reached. Thus when we have the first inklings that there *is* a real Self, we begin to search for it, as if it or we were lost. We ask, "How can I come to know the real Self?" This is to be asleep to who we really are.

When we awaken from the sleep state of objective

consciousness (called "maya" in Eastern philosophies, "illusion" in esoteric traditions, and "waking dreams" in more current descriptions), we recover or reclaim our consciousness *as the real Self.* We "remember" who we are.

There is only one Self. What changes, awakens, develops, and unfolds is our *knowing* of Self. At each stage we are identified with only a portion of the total Self. The sense of "I" is limited. It is the sense of "I" that expands as we come to know more of the Self that we are.

What Is It Like To Be Awakened?

To awaken is to fulfill our potential as human beings and to be born into a new realm. In the past, persons still functioning in objective consciousness viewed awakened Beings as gods. This suggested that they no longer seemed human and were outside the range of what is possible for the ordinary person. Yet among those who are awakened, there are children as well as adults, for to awaken is not only to culminate the human phase of emergence, but it is to begin a whole new phase of unfolding in realms of consciousness that are so vast as to be unimaginable from our present stage of development. Thus a god, so called by a person functioning in objective consciousness, may be only a child among awakened or enlightened Beings.

A similar phenomenon occurs in the other phases of evolution. Although we speak of the mineral kingdom, the plant kingdom and the animal kingdom, scientists are not able to say precisely where one kingdom ends and the other begins. The transition is gradual and the lines we draw between them are arbitrary. Crystals, for example, are very highly developed minerals that come so close to being plants that some scientists feel they should be classified as such. Yet among plants, crystals surely seem primitive, or childlike. They are quite rigid and fixed in their Self-expression, lacking the plasticity of other species in the plant kingdom.

In the transition from plant to animal, a sea anemone appears to be a plant, because it prefers to remain "rooted" or fixed in place as most plants do. Yet the sea anemone has developed certain kinds of mobility, sensitivity and digestive processes that are more characteristic of animals than plants. Compared to a whale or dolphin, however, the sea anemone would surely be recognized as a very primitive, or childlike, marine animal.

The line between animals and humans is no clearer. Apes, monkeys, and chimpanzees have long been thought to resemble human beings, but they remain classified as animals. Some human children, on the other hand, are so severely retarded, as we say, that they hardly seem human.

Thus it seems safe to say that there is no distinct delineation between humans and the species we become when we are fully individualized. The gods of Greek and Roman mythology exhibited many human characteristics, such as falling in love, losing their tempers, and experiencing jealousy, and yet they had powers beyond what humans usually exhibit. Surely when we awaken, we will still have many human characteristics, even though our consciousness will have expanded and we will know that we are "new."

Every final point in one cycle of unfolding becomes a new beginning in another realm of consciousness. At each stage along the way, we *lose* one sense of self in order to find a more all-encompassing one, but **the new always incorporates the old**. Thus to awaken will be like be-

The Process of Awakening 53

ing entirely different, yet also very much the same.

When the Self emerged as mineral, It incorporated the molecular level of development and made it more complex. When the Self emerged as plant, It incorporated minerals into Its organism, endowing them with new plasticity and a greater capacity to change. Because their growth and change are easily observed, we consider them to be alive.

When the Self emerged as animal, It incorporated the plasticity of plants into increasingly complex bodily tissues and endowed animals with a capacity to change that is so rapid that we call it movement. Animals expanded their responsiveness to their environment, utilizing movement to ensure their survival. Plants breathed, in the sense of taking in carbon dioxide and breathing out oxygen into the atmosphere around them, but animals developed lungs that made breathing a more sharply defined function. The breath together with new sensory responses made it possible for animals to feel rudimentary emotions and to develop embryonic psyches, or souls.

When the Self emerged as human, It incorporated the mobility, the breath, and the emotional sensitivity of the animal and elaborated them. The faculty of self-consciousness emerged and a sense of "I" accompanied it. Humans grew their mental capacities until they could remember personal history and develop reason. These new human faculties made it possible to begin the second movement of the creating process: the unfolding of consciousness from within form.

When the Self emerges as more-than-human, It incorporates the reasoning power and memory of the human and expands them so that the "I" of the human encompasses the whole dynamic Creative Force. Thus awakened Beings emerge as co-creators with the original Creative Force. That process of expansion will continue until the Self knows Itself as All That Is.

I slept in stone

I dreamed as a flower

As an animal I awoke

But my own Self

I never knew

Until I came

To live with you.

–Rumi
12th Century

When we will have fully awakened, we will know ourselves as cells in the body of the One, the Whole. We will know our unique places in the overall pattern of life. We will each know that there is no death. We will recognize every person, including self, as an essential part of the Whole with a vital function to fulfill, and therefore as a being of infinite worth. We will see the Whole of life as an intricate web and know that we are each linked to all other facets of the energy world – human, animal, vegetable, mineral – in such a delicate balance that no facet of the Whole can be ignored. We will recognize our capacity as conscious Beings to strengthen the cohesion and unity of the Whole through the binding power of Universal Love. That will constitute a great liberation.

One of the wise philosophers has said, '... a wise man should strive after a knowledge of Self; for there is no knowledge that is higher, or that brings more satisfaction of power, than a knowledge of his own being.' If a man knows his real Self, he cannot do otherwise than discover his latent possibilities, his concealed powers, his dormant faculties. Of what avail, if a man should 'gain the whole world and lose his own soul'? His soul is his spiritual self, and if he truly discovers his spiritual self he can build a whole world if he is serving his fellow men by so doing. I have learned that he who would attain the ultimate goal must search the depths of this real Self, and there he will find God, the fullness of all good.

– *Baird T. Spalding*

Chapter Five

THE HUMAN SLEEP STATE: OBJECTIVE CONSCIOUSNESS AND IDENTIFICATION WITH THE PHYSICAL BODY

In order to fully understand the process of awakening, we must first understand our sleep-state. The ordinary human state of consciousness is an objective self-consciousness. With self-consciousness we took the first step out of group identity; yet relative to the awakened state, we are still asleep. We are no longer in the deepest sleep state, however, as are minerals, plants, and animals. We humans have begun to have waking dreams.

How Does Objective Self-Consciousness Differ From The Animal State Of Consciousness?

Animals are totally identified with the groups (species or sub-species) to which they belong. A horse never suffers the confusion of thinking it might be a cat, for instance. Animals are governed by group patterns held in the energy field corresponding to that group. Those patterns motivate animals on an unconscious level through instinct. For example, a horse whinnies; it doesn't meow;

it gallops but doesn't prowl. Animals have no sense of "I." They cannot think of themselves or for themselves. And no animal has yet developed an abstract representation of itself or its group — as in drawings or paintings — or of their thought processes — as in writing. An individual animal is truly only a representative of the group to which it belongs.

Occasionally we read a story about an animal that has crossed into another animal group field for a time. For example, a mother dog might nurse a cat that has been abandoned by its mother until the cat is old enough to be weaned. Nevertheless, the cat will behave like a cat, not a dog. It will make cat sounds, not dog sounds. It will continue to conform to its own species' group field even though it has been nurtured for a time by a different animal. Animals cannot cross over into different animal fields. They represent a group field rather than an individualized expression of Self.

The story of the Ugly Duckling illustrates this point. A baby swan was raised by a mother duck along with her other ducklings. As the little ones grew, the swan grew too fast and too large. It became an unsightly, ugly duckling, who seemed awkward and distorted by comparison with the ducks. It was not capable of becoming a duck even if it wanted to. Then one day some swans came along and the ugly duckling saw that it belonged with them. It was not an ugly duckling; it was a beautiful swan. It came to know itself by finding the group field in which it was integrated and of which it was a reflection. Then it felt at home because it was like the other swans.

Primitive human beings functioned as "we" without a sense of "I." But they began to develop symbolic language and, with it, the ability to think. Thinking is a process of abstracting – that is, of being able to hold a picture-image of an event past the moment of its occurrence. That seemingly simple process of abstracting an image from an event and holding it in consciousness enables humans to think.

Once humans developed the ability to think, we could think not only about the world around us, but also about self. Thus, the ability to think enabled us to develop a consciousness of self, or self-consciousness. We began to hold images of ourselves as objects among other objects in the world around us. We could distinguish between the activities of the groups to which we belonged and our own acts, because we could remember what we had done and why. We could think private thoughts. This distinguishes our consciousness from that of the animals.

What Are Waking Dreams?

When we, as human beings, became conscious of ourselves as separate from the group, we began to develop autonomous fields, or to undergo the individualizing process. To stay with the analogy of sleeping and waking, we began to dream waking dreams which were ours alone. In those waking dreams, we believed ourselves to be awake. The waking dreams were so vivid that we believed we *were* the pictures of self we saw in the waking dream state, rather than knowing that we were the ones who were dreaming. Believing the images of the waking dream state to be real, we called the images in our waking dreams "real life."[7]

These waking dreams enable us to be conscious of ourselves as individuals, and it is this consciousness that

---

[7] For further elaboration of this metaphor, see *Life As A Waking Dream* by Diane Kennedy Pike.

builds an autonomous field. A sense of "I" leads to awareness of ownership, and we begin to say "this object is mine, and that one is yours." A waking dream image of self causes us to identify with certain qualities of being, skills, and abilities, and we begin to think: "I am tall, strong, athletic, responsible, smart, and friendly." Or, "I am inept, ugly, an outcast, and unlucky." In our consciousness we grasp hold of those characteristics and use them to construct an image of self that forms our identity. We say, "I'm the kind of person who," or "that's the way I am." Though we are still asleep, by identifying what we are like and how we are different from others we begin to build the individualized fields in which we will one day awaken to live our lives as conscious cells in the body of the Whole.

What Is An Autonomous Field?

I liken the individualized fields we build in our unconsciousness to the shells of chicken eggs. Each shell contains within it the substance out of which a baby chick will develop. The human psyche or soul is like the albumen of the egg. It is the stuff that nurtures the emerging new self. While still in the shell, the fetus takes the form of a chicken, though it is not yet living and breathing on its own. The mother hen keeps it warm until it has developed sufficiently to pip its shell.

Likewise, the groups in which human beings grow up keep the developing individual alive by giving it a sense of belonging and of being loved. Meanwhile, it grows a shell of self-identity (a personality, psyche, or soul) that for the time being seems to separate it from others. But the sense of being increasingly different from others also protects the fetal individual until it is strong enough to function as a unit unto itself. Then it begins to pip the shell of objective consciousness. The pipping is the process of awakening.

When the chick emerges from the egg shell, it has enough strength to live on its own. Likewise, when we awaken to know ourselves as microcosmic expressions of the One Self, we have built energy fields that can be entirely autonomous. That is, they do not have to be held and sustained by any given group field. They are nourished directly by the cosmic field in which all autonomous fields are integrated. Each individual is whole in self (not capable of being divided) and able to function as a conscious unit within the larger Whole.

What Are Some Examples Of Waking Dreams Within Our Objective State Of Consciousness?

Objective self-consciousness, or real life as most humans know it, is characterized by a sense of self as an object separate from other objects in the world around. From the inside of the autonomous fields we are building (our "egg shells"), we come to know the world around us through images held in our psyches . We think about our experiences by reviewing those pictures and the feelings that accompanied them. Then we develop a story about the images to make sense out of our responses. These stories are what I call waking dreams.

Here's an example. Rita was developing a sense of herself as different from other members of her family. She often felt she didn't belong to them and even wondered if she had been adopted. One day when she was 12, she began to menstruate. She took her soiled panties to her mother and told her that she had begun her period. Her mother looked shocked, grabbed the panties, and said, "Oh my god, I had no idea." She turned away from Rita.

Rita took the image of her mother's shocked expression into her psyche and told herself this story: "I have done it wrong again. I should never have told her. She thinks I am a freak. She can't even stand to look at me." Then she ran to her room and flung herself on her bed, crying. This incident only reinforced Rita's conviction that she did not belong in that family.

Meanwhile, her mother was inside her shell telling herself this story: "I thought I had plenty of time to tell Rita about menstruation. I had no idea she would begin her period so soon. I am a terrible mother. I have failed my daughter at the time she needs me most. How can I ever make this right?" Rita's mother had turned from her out of embarrassment and shame that *she* had done it wrong, not because she thought there was something wrong with Rita.

Mother and daughter, each in her own shell, each living her own waking dream, were unable to communicate with one another because of their preoccupation with the images in their psyches and the stories they developed around them. They were immersed in their waking dreams.

Why Do We Function In Objective Consciousness If This Is Really An Energy World?

While functioning totally in objective consciousness, we identify with our physical forms since that is the image we hold of ourselves. We look at our bodies in a mirror and think, "That is what *I* look like." If asked what personal space we occupy, we point to the outline of our skins. We feel we are defined by the parameters of our bodies.

Objects, or more accurately, images held in our psyches that appear to be substantive and thus objective, do not exist except in the waking dream state. When we awaken, we discover a dynamic energy world in which there are no objects. Why, then, do we experience the world this way while we are in our waking dreams?

The neural system of the vast majority of human beings is not capable of registering the interstices between the rapidly swirling atoms that compose every "thing" in the world around us, including our bodies. Instead of seeing a mass of swirling, dynamic energy, most of us perceive only the outline of the pathways the particles of energy are traveling, and from that outline we form an image in our consciousness. We fill in the outline with the interpretation we have been taught. Thus we might say, "That is a tree." That interpretation of the image represents a group consensus that enables us to communicate with others. Sometimes we add our own preferences and judgments to the group interpretation. We might say, for example, "That is an ugly tree." The assessment "ugly" reflects our evaluation of the tree we are seeing. It is not a statement about the tree itself.

The image in our psyches appears solid to us, when in fact the image does not exist except in our psyche. Since the psyche is composed of astral substance, the image held in it cannot be made of physical matter. But the tree itself, which the image represents, is not solid either. The image in our psyche is like a digital representation of the tree, and the tree itself is an energy field that is constantly moving, vibrating, pulsating, changing, like pinpoints of light that form the pattern of what we call "tree."

Most of us are not conscious of the limitations of our nervous systems, nor are we conscious of the abstracting process by which we form images that look solid to us. Consequently, we assume that *what we see* (namely, our mental images-appearing-solid) *is* the reality. We identify the image with the reality. I *see* a solid table; therefore, I reason, the table is solid.

The same phenomenon occurs with the sense of touch. When the surface of our skin touches another surface, our nervous system cannot register the interstices between the molecules of energy forming the energy field we have encountered. The surface seems impenetrable, or solid. Moreover, the outline of our own skin with which we have touched the table also seems to have a relatively firm and impenetrable surface. This is because, again, our neural system cannot register the individual molecules that make up our skin. We generalize what we are feeling and imagine our skin to be a surface that encloses us.

We know with our rational thought processes that skin is not impenetrable, because it can be cut open or punctured with a needle or a pin. Even wood or cement or brick can be penetrated if an object, like a nail, is strong enough. Nevertheless, we think of these objects as solid and we relate to them that way. The illusion is reinforced when we fall and get a bruise from the encounter.

Why Is This Illusion A Problem? Why Is It Important To Awaken From Waking Dreams?

Though mental images are *abstracted from* the energy reality and only *represent our human experience of the energy*, most of us interact with the world around us as though those images *were* the reality. We live as though solid objects surround us, and as though *we* are objects (namely, the physical body). Thus we speak of "bumping into" a door or a wall, of "stepping on" the grass, of "picking up" a glass, etc. We relate to our *images* of the reality rather than to the dynamic energy systems themselves, cutting ourselves off from the *real* to relate instead to our *impressions* of the real.

As a consequence, when we walk through a building, we imagine that we emerge unchanged and that the building has not been impacted by our presence. After all, we reason falsely, we traversed a "space" which the building surrounded, our shoes protected us from touching the floor, and the doors opened and closed automatically. We are completely unaware that we actually commingled with the molecules of the building, and we are ignorant of the effect that had on us.

One time in Chicago, at a time when I was highly sensitized by the process of awakening going on in my field, I came up out of the subway into the vast lobby of a large office building. The marble was so alive that it came to meet me as I walked through the lobby. I was almost dizzy with the sensation of being enveloped in living marble. It was intense and oppressive. When I stepped out onto the sidewalk it was as if I had left an embrace that had been so imposing that I was glad to be free of it. It was in that moment I realized how unaware I usually am of the effect a building has on me. And I realized that by my presence I had left an impression on the marble, though I had no way to assess the difference I had made.

In that instance, I had not merely looked at my images of the marble with which the lobby was constructed, I had experienced consciously the energetic impact it made on me. Had I passed through that lobby every day, I would either have become stronger in order to withstand it, or I would have begun to feel diminished, if not crushed, by it. I wondered how many of the workers were aware of the building's effect on them.

We are isolated in our private, mental worlds of objective self-consciousness, but we do not know it. We are confined to waking dreams, but we call them real life. This private mental world is called *maya* in the Eastern traditions and *illusion* in Western traditions of the Wisdom. It is the reality pointed to by the terms "the Devil," "the power of evil," and "the father of all lies" in the Christian tradition, for it is what causes us to separate ourselves from others and from God, resulting in the condition called sin.

Because we are unconscious of *how* we function, we are actually *deceived by* the way we function. No wonder we are often so puzzled by the behavior of others and frustrated with what appears to be our own ineffectiveness in the world. We try to communicate with others, not realizing that we are living one waking dream and they are living another. This causes us great distress and suffering.

What Can We Do About This Problem If We Have Not Yet Awakened?

To begin to break free, we first need to become conscious of the process of abstracting so that we no longer confuse our *images* of the energy world, which appear solid but actually exist only in our mental processes, with the energy world itself. A study of General Semantics enables us to make that distinction.

The purpose of learning to abstract consciously is to free our consciousness for more expansive realization. It is not that we will no longer abstract from the dynamic energy world, or that images will no longer appear solid in our consciousness. *We will continue to have private mental worlds in which we create our waking dreams and call them real life* long into the process of awakening.

Instead, we can become so conscious of the *process* by which we create our private worlds that they will no longer imprison us. We will become conscious not only of our private worlds, but also of the energy world itself and how we function in it. We will be *conscious* of the waking dream world we once believed to be real life while *also* being conscious of the energy world.

In addition, we can learn to use our waking dreams to teach us the next steps we need to take in the energy world. I have come to view waking dreams as the language that the Great Mother uses for communication with us.[8] The more we learn to understand the language of symbolism, the more we will be able to see the deeper meaning behind our everyday experiences which we live as waking dreams.

The objective state of consciousness, then, is a stage in the development of the human being. During this phase, we are still too embryonic on the physiological level to awaken to the energy world. We are like newborn kittens whose eyes remain closed until our organisms develop enough to handle the influx of light that will come when the eyelids open. We are like chicks still inside their shells, not strong enough yet to pip them and step into the energy world. Human consciousness in this objective phase is limited to images and interpretations of the world in which we live. We are unable to be conscious of the energy world as it is.

---

[8] See *Life As A Waking Dream,* chapter nine.

How Does Objective Consciousness Affect The Way We Know Ourselves?

In the objective state of consciousness, we are conscious of ourselves *as* our bodies. Thus, whatever happens to our bodies, we experience as happening to us. We say, "You hit me," whereas the blow was actually to the body; "I am sick," when referring to a condition of disease in the body; and "I am growing old," even though only the body conforms to the laws of aging and decay that characterize the physical world.

When we identify with our bodies, we live in a constant sense of separation, isolation, and loneliness. No other body can, by definition, share the space occupied by my body. No degree of sharing or intimacy with another can dissolve the barrier to union, for the barrier is in our consciousness where we see ourselves as impenetrable, irrevocably contained, objects. When we perceive ourselves as confined within the boundaries of our bodies, there is no way to experience total union with another. We are isolated within our identification with our bodies, within our sense of ourselves as bodies.

When we are identified with our bodies, we think that by changing our bodies we change ourselves. To deal with "I am fat," we diet. But "I am thin" is not easy to maintain when only the body has been changed. To deal with "I am unattractive," we apply make-up, have plastic surgery, or buy stylish clothes. The body may look better by societal standards, but the amount of maintenance required belies any real change, and often we still do not *feel* more attractive.

When we are identified with our bodies, we think we interact with the world around us only through our five physical senses. Moreover, we think our senses function *in* the body. We must see, touch, or hear something before we are convinced it is real and we distrust whatever cannot be established by sensory confirmation. It seems impossible to one in objective consciousness that a person without a body could sense anything. Yet we experience a lack of physical sensation under hypnosis or anesthesia when, though the body is clearly still alive, our consciousness is detached from it. If the sensing were in the *body*, a live body would continue to feel no matter what. That a body can live and yet lose its senses indicates that the sensing is in our consciousness, not in the body.

When identified with the body, we doubt any reality we cannot touch, taste, smell, hear, or see, yet our physical senses cannot touch, taste, smell, hear, or see *the consciousness with which we doubt.*

Is There Any Hope For Us?

When we are identified with our bodies, we are only one step removed from the state of consciousness represented by the animal world. Animals *appear* to function in objective consciousness, but they are not conscious of themselves as they function. We humans observe ourselves as we function. We *perceive* ourselves as objects. We *think about ourselves*, as though we were separate from ourselves. We are conscious of ourselves, or *self-conscious.* We *think* we are bound, limited and restricted to the physical realm, yet because we are thinking, we already transcend the physical.

Because we are self-conscious, we are able to examine our lives and make new choices. If we catch a glimpse of the More that awaits us, we are able to opt for the More. We have the capacity to comprehend the limitations of our objective consciousness and to expand beyond it.

Because we are self-conscious, we can experience restlessness and respond to the driving force from within which urges us to unfold, to fulfill our potential. We can become seekers. We can choose to cooperate consciously with the developmental pattern of our own inner being.

Because we are self-conscious, we can set out on the spiritual journey into Self, which will lead to our awakening. In our awareness of our limitation lies the key to our freedom.

Chapter Six

PHASE ONE OF THE AWAKENING: IDENTIFYING WITH THE PERSONALITY

Even while we are still asleep, dreaming waking dreams which we think of as real, we have already begun to awaken. Our consciousness of self and our ability to reason are evidence that the seed of the real Self within has begun to germinate. This first phase of the process of awakening is comparable to being aware that we are dreaming just before we awaken from the dream.

Soon we begin to acknowledge that we are more than our bodies – that we are also feelings, thoughts, and patterns of behavior and interaction that make us identifiable in many more ways than just how we look. We discover our psyches, first in the form of our personalities and later as the more expansive capacities of the unconscious.

When we speak of our personalities, we are usually referring to the way other people see us and know us, or at least to how we *believe* they see us and know us. The word comes from the Greek word "persona," which means "mask." It is good to keep this in mind, since the personality may hide as much as it expresses of the consciousness behind it. Sometimes in order to know ourselves better, we actually ask other people, "How do you see me?" We form images in our psyches based on how we experience ourselves and how we think others experience us. Then we identify with those images and claim them as our personality, as "who we are." Eventually we come to know more than just this "persona." We learn to understand the psyche and the laws by which it functions.

The discovery that we are *also* a personality is a crack in our objective identification, for we cannot with our physical senses see, touch, taste, smell, or hear feelings and thoughts. Feelings, thoughts, memories, and habit patterns occupy no identifiable space, and have no clear boundaries that would make apparent their separateness from the feelings and thoughts of other persons. When we become conscious of our personalities, even though the habit may linger of thinking of ourselves as confined to a body, we have in fact broken out of total identification with the body. We are stirring in our sleep and have begun to awaken.

When Do We Usually Begin To Identify With The Personality?

For many people, awareness of the personality as a primary way of knowing themselves begins during their teen years. Those are the years when we want desperately to belong to a group. We do our best to conform. We wear clothes and hairstyles that make us *look* like our friends. We adopt words, phrases, and expressions that make us *sound* like our friends. We even adopt the attitudes, moods, and behaviors that prevail in our chosen group of friends.

However, all of that is not enough to make us feel secure in our identity with a group when we become aware of our personalities. Awareness of the qualities that make up our personalities constitutes further individualization, or differentiation from the group. We begin to see that not only do we have bodies separate from other bodies, but also we have personalities different from all other personalities. Our sense of self as unique and individual grows, even though we may still be governed primarily by group patterns in our personality expression.

People who have not yet begun to seek – that is, to long for an understanding of the natural order process – are often afraid of the ways they are different from others. They are afraid that if they stand out as unique, they will no longer be included in the group and thus will be alone and lonely. They are afraid that if their friends find out what they are really like, no one will want to be around them any more, let alone like or love them. Consequently, these people try to hide those characteristics that they believe to be unacceptable or unlovable. They think something is wrong with them and they don't want anyone to find that out. Such fears often make the teen years particularly difficult, but they can arise at any age.

But those who are stirring in their sleep cannot go back and blend in with the crowd. Their awareness that they are different persists, and with it may come the fear that they will *never* belong, that no one will ever really understand them. This phase of the awakening process can be very painful. It is a little bit like struggling to wake up from a nightmare at night.

It is precisely that feeling of uniqueness that prompts the real Self to stir within us. Therefore that feeling, even with the pain it sometimes brings, is essential to the process of awakening. Eventually it prompts us to seek to understand ourselves and our uniqueness.

To return to the analogy of the chicken in its shell, the discomfort of feeling unique is a signal to the growing self that it is time to pip the shell of objective identity.

How Can We Grow In Our Understanding Of Ourselves?

The first indication that the sleeping Self has begun to stir comes in a growing desire to know and understand ourselves. The science of psychology developed in response to that very urge in our group psyche. The urge to examine the self, and to understand the inner workings of the human psyche, has been powerful in Western culture since the beginning of the twentieth century. It has led to astonishing changes in social institutions like marriage and in customs regarding social interactions, such as addressing authority figures by their first names instead of using Mr. and Mrs.

Psychology was built on a medical model of seeking to cure illnesses. Consequently, those who seek psychological help usually do so because they are afraid there is something wrong with them. In effect, they want to be "cured" of their perception that they are different from other people. Or they hope the therapist will be able to change the characteristics they believe to be unlovable.

Some do not seek psychological help precisely because they are afraid of what they will discover if they engage in self-examination. They are reluctant to uncover facets of self of which they are not yet aware, for fear they cannot be made "normal" again and be like others. They are often also afraid of the changes that might ensue from greater self-awareness. Such fear creates inner conflicts and disturbances that then trouble them further.

In effect, many who seek psychological help are, at least in the beginning, hoping someone can help stop the process of awakening that is occurring within.

Is Everyone Who Seeks A Psychotherapist Awakening?

Perhaps not everyone that goes into psychotherapy is beginning to awaken, but I believe that most are. People reach out to psychologists hoping to get help so they can live their lives with greater skill, whether they are in phase one, two, or three of the process of awakening. How the therapist responds to this cry for help depends largely on the phase of his or her own unfolding consciousness.

Some psychologists and therapists do their best to glue their clients' objective self-consciousness back together. Others help clients move past their fears so they can begin to know the undisclosed Self. Analysts engage their clients for years in an examination of their early lives in an attempt to understand why they are the way they are. Increasingly, both psychiatrists and psychologists seek to restore balance in many clients by prescribing psychotropic drugs.

Although such therapy can help to relieve inner pressure for a time, if the individual is beginning to awaken, the pressure will return. In fact, the pressure is an indication of a very natural process at work within. Pressure is how we experience the urge to grow, the urge to expand our consciousness. Qabalists use "pressure" as a way to describe God: God is pressure at work in us and in the cosmos.

A growing number of therapists of different backgrounds and training are beginning to trust the process of unfolding consciousness, even if they don't have a simple overview such as I am presenting here. All of them, it seems to me, are at least in phase one of the awakening process, aware that it is important to recognize and understand the personality but perhaps not yet in possession of a larger understanding of the individualizing process. Only those who have received spiritual instruction in this or a previous life will be able to reassure their clients that inner pressure and the conflicts that arise because of it are the natural consequences of a universal process of coming to know the real Self.

What If We're *Not* Afraid To Be Unique?

Even when we *welcome* the process of awakening, we sometimes feel apprehension about the unknown. But we also feel eagerness and excitement. We have a sense of urgency about getting on with the process we are in and often feel that if we don't get help, we will die. We don't want to die; we want to live. Thus we reach out for help.

When we seek therapy out of eagerness to know rather than out of fear, a therapist will be able to help us much more quickly. Most therapists and counselors are very good at guiding people to learn more about themselves and to understand how their psyches work. The absence of resistance not only makes us more open to the person to whom we reach out, it also makes us more open to what we will uncover in self. That is a great boon.

If we are awakening and we neither resist nor pursue the process, we tend to welcome information about our personalities when we come across it. We are often drawn to what is called popular psychology. We will read self-help books and attend lectures, seminars, workshops, and conferences focused on understanding ourselves and learning techniques for greater self-control.

This first phase in the process of awakening, then,

could be called a psychological stage. Psychology means knowledge of the psyche. If we are drawn to psychology in whatever form it is because the urge to know ourselves as personalities has motivated us. We might remain in that stage of the awakening process for the rest of this lifetime.

Doesn't The Body Need To Be Included In This Self-Examination?

The key thing to understand, if you want an overview of the process of awakening, is that during the early stages we discover that we are not *just* a physical body. We are far more complex than we first believed. Our bodies are affected by our feelings and thoughts. Our feelings and thoughts are intertwined in complex patterns. We have developed habit patterns of response and those patterns repeat themselves automatically without our conscious volition. In effect, we discover that "who we are" is a series of patterns of feelings, thoughts, actions, and reactions that have become identifiable and predictable. We know we are living in bodies, but we have also become aware of our personalities.

In the realm of medicine, the traditional pattern of (1) diagnosis of illness, followed by (2) surgery, or (3) chemical cures for the symptoms, reflects the objective state of consciousness and serves the needs of persons identified with their bodies. "If you cure my body, 'I' will be well."

Today, the expanding awareness of self as a personality is reflected in the growing holistic approach to medicine. Practitioners are attempting to relate to the complexities of a being composed of body, thoughts, and emotions. They seek not only to treat symptoms, but also to find out causes. They enlist their patients, in whom the urge to know Self is growing, in their efforts not only to heal dis-ease when they encounter it, but also to prevent new imbalance before it occurs.

As we shall see, however, there is far more to discover before medicine will be truly holistic. At present, holistic medicine addresses the Self primarily in its earliest stages of awakening.

What Is The True Structure Of The Human?

The Wisdom teaches us that humans are microcosmic reflections of the Original One. Like the First Principle described in Part One under the Sacred Science, the triune real Self of the individual human expresses through the Lower Quaternary, known as the mental, emotional, etheric, and physical bodies. However, in the early stages of our awakening, we are not conscious of any distinction between the physical and the etheric bodies. And as we become conscious of our personalities, we initially think of them primarily as patterns and characteristics.

We say things like, "I am the kind of person who is always late," "I am an impatient person," or "I am outgoing," or "I am an addict," or "I am a hard worker." Since we do not see beyond the patterns, we feel helpless to change them. "There's nothing I can do. That's the way I am," we loudly assert. "You're asking me to change *who I am*," or "I can only be myself."

We are totally identified with the personality patterns we discover as we begin to awaken, and we tend to attribute any change that *does* occur to an outside, often Divine, source. "I am helpless to change myself, but *God* intervened and saved me from my uncontrollable anger."

We can only account for change by attributing power to an outside force because we do not yet know ourselves as anything more than the patterns. We don't understand the complexities of the psyche or the larger structure of the Self.

Early in this first phase of awakening, however, we begin to distinguish between three fundamental facets of the self: body, feelings and thoughts. When we bring into consciousness the dynamic interaction between these three facets of self, we are better able to cope with, and even to choose, change.

How Do Bodies Speak?

Most of us are initially more conscious of our bodies than we are of our feelings and thoughts. We can help to awaken ourselves by looking in the mirror of our physical bodies to identify patterns of feeling and thinking.

For example, a stomach "tied in knots" may indicate an experience that was distasteful, disagreeable and unpalatable that we have refused to digest, or integrate. A stiff neck may reflect stubbornness, or a refusal to adapt or bend. A strained back may reveal that we are carrying too much responsibility or that we have deep feelings that are too heavy to bear. A sore toe may be the result of putting our foot down too hard – or of hesitating to put it down at all.

Physical bodies, we discover, reflect our feelings, thoughts, and life-long patterns. Physical bodies speak to us in the only mode of communication they have at their disposal: *They take on the "form" of the feelings, thoughts, and/or habit patterns.* Many body workers (massage therapists, energy healers, etc.) are good at helping their clients to understand what their bodies are communicating through the discomfort or pain of physical conditions. By learning the symbolic or metaphorical language of our physical bodies, we can expand our consciousness of feelings and thoughts.

Are Feelings In The Body?

Our awareness of sensation is made possible by our etheric bodies, which are "doubles" of our physical bodies. The etheric body is made of astral rather than material substance, and it adheres to the pattern of the physical body. The energy impulses of the physical world are transmitted through our nerve channels to the brain where our *consciousness* interprets them. This interpretation occurs in the etheric body, which acts as an intermediary between the physical body and the emotional and mental bodies.

In our emotional bodies, we become conscious of sensations that are not transmitted by the physical senses, namely, feelings of pleasure and pain. At first we might think that it is the physical body that experiences all sensation. However, if we think about it we discover it is not so. For example, the sense of touch seems to be in the physical body. However, a light touch might bring one person pleasure ("That feels so good; just like a feather!") and another pain ("I can't stand that! It tickles!"). And a third person, concentrating on a book or watching an exciting sports event on television, might not even notice the light touch! So contact with the body doesn't determine whether we notice a sensation or whether we experience pleasure or pain. Those sensations are determined in the psyche, which encompasses the etheric, emotional, and mental bodies.

I have heard many women describe the experience of being sexually violated. Often they report that they left their bodies during the experience. In those instances, the women felt no pain during the attack on their physical bodies. "It was as if I was watching from a distance, waiting for it to be over." Since the registry of sensation and of pleasure and pain are in the consciousness of "I," to dissociate from the body, that is, not to remain identified with it, is to avoid experiencing the impact of the rape.

In the case of being sexually violated, the shock of the event may have precipitated the dissociation. Another way of dissociating from the experience of the body is to dull the nerves that transmit impulses to the brain. That is what anesthetics do. Still another way is through hypnosis, whether self-induced or suggested by another. In that case the individual turns his/her attention away from the sensations that are being registered, to focus on something else. A hypnotist gives the subject something to look at (perhaps a swinging pendulum) and thoughts to concentrate on (you are feeling very sleepy; you are very relaxed; you will remember nothing). In autosuggestion, you give yourself something to focus on, such as the memory of a beautiful scene, a prayer, a mantra, or thoughts of another time or place. Such images or thoughts occupy your awareness so that you are no longer identified with the body. Trances induced by repetitive movements and/or chanted sounds can have a similar effect.

In all these cases, the individual is not identified with what is happening to the body and therefore experiences no pain or pleasure. The etheric body does not transmit the nerve impulses from the physical to the astral. People can walk on hot coals of fire or lie on beds of nails and not experience pain even though their feet get blistered and their skin is punctured. Or, as in the first example, a woman can be brutally raped and not remember the pain or the shame of it because, in fact, she didn't experience it.

But the reverse can also occur. By calling up an image of an event, or by reentering it in memory and inviting a registry of the sensations, we can go back to a past event and live the experience as if it were happening now. The etheric body, which is not bound by time and space, picks up the energy of the event and transmits it to the emotional body as if it were occurring in the present moment. The resultant waking dream can provide us with symbols and metaphors to develop our understanding of life and the implications of experiences.[9]

Do These Experiences Help Form Our Personalities?

As a result of registering pleasure and pain, we polarize our experience of the world around us, and the world within, according to what we like (what brings us pleasure) and what we dislike (what brings us pain). At the polar extremes we say we "love" some persons and things and "hate" others. And toward the middle of the spectrum we indicate preferences for or against.

How we "feel" about a life experience or a personal interaction determines whether we will pursue it or turn (perhaps run) away from it. The spectrum of preferences

---

[9] In Waking Dream classes or coaching sessions, we work with such life experiences to penetrate their deeper meaning. You can also do this work yourself, but it is often helpful to have someone facilitate your work who is a step beyond you in the process of awakening.

we develop helps to define our personality pattern. For example, falling through space can take your breath away. Some people find that experience exciting and pleasureful. They may choose skydiving as a recreational pursuit, or they may enjoy going on carnival rides like the free fall or the roller coaster. Other people may be terrified of falling through space and find even the thought of it painful. Those people are more likely to pursue entertainment that keeps their feet on the ground, like golf or bridge.

When describing the difference in the personalities of these contrasting responses to falling through space, we might call one brave or foolhardy and the other cautious and sensible. In other words, one of the ways we characterize personalities is according to their likes and dislikes, what brings them pleasure and what brings them pain.

In addition, *values* are based on these personal, experiential preferences. For instance, some people find arguments and disagreements stimulating and enjoyable; others experience them as very difficult and even painful. The former might place a high value on the open expression of opinions, direct communication of criticism, and heated debate before making decisions or taking action. The latter might value indirect communication in order not to arouse strong reactions, and compromise rather than trying to work out differences. Since we tend to *feel strongly* about the value systems we develop, it is easy to recognize how important the registry of pleasure and pain is in the development of our personalities.

In this initial phase of the process of awakening, to become conscious of our feelings is an important part of coming to know and understand the personality we have developed. The more aware we become of our feelings, the less identified with them we will be. In the second phase of our awakening, we will go deeper and discover that feelings in the psyche can serve as a conduit for our awareness of spirit.

What Part Do Our Thoughts Play In This?

It is in the mental body that we are able to capture images of our experiences and hold them in much the same way as cameras record images. The images held in the psyche in astral substance make it possible for us to think about our experiences. It is here that we engage in the process of abstraction, using words to label the images. We also develop reasoning or logic, which involves higher order abstractions. It is in the objective mind that we are at this very moment, to a greater or lesser degree, communicating with one another via the written word. "Thinking" is a complex process that few come to genuinely understand. Yet such understanding is essential to our awakening.

Part of the difficulty with understanding our thinking processes is that we try to *use* the mind to examine the mind. To think about thoughts gets us about as far as a dog gets when it tries to catch its own tail. When we think about our thoughts we experience something like a conversation between various "voices" in our heads. They are not actual voices, but one thought will say, "Why do you always take a negative view of every situation?" Another thought will respond: "You're generalizing. I don't *always* do *anything*. But I do at least try to be realistic." Perhaps a third "voice" jumps in: "It doesn't really matter what you think or how you think because nothing is going to change anyway. This situation is hopeless." "There you go again," says voice #2. And so the conversation continues.

In fact, to begin to understand the workings of the mind, we must expand into the finer frequencies of the real Self, or spirit. It is perhaps for that reason that thoughts are often referred to as the "lower mind" or the "objective mind." If there were no "higher mind" we would not be able to observe and reason about our mental processes.

As we develop awareness of the personality and of the interaction between the physical body and our feelings and thoughts, we have already begun to cross over from the first to the second phase of the process of awakening.

What Are Private Worlds?

To grasp how thoughts and feelings contribute to our personality patterns, we need to understand the concept of private worlds.

Private worlds[10] are comparable to edited videotapes of our life experiences, run with interpretive commentary. Whenever we have an experience, we select images from the experience that particularly impress us. We store those images, the feelings that accompanied them, and our thoughts about what the experience meant to us.

For example. You are seated at the dining room table with your family. Conversation is lively, but you are listening with only half your attention. Your mind has wandered. Suddenly you realize that someone has spoken directly to you. You snap to attention, but have not heard the question. Your brother says, "What's wrong

---

[10] I am indebted to Vitvan, my teacher, for this term "private world." and for his description of it.

Figure 1: OBJECTIVE IDENTITY

THE PRIVATE WORLD
(nonfunctional)

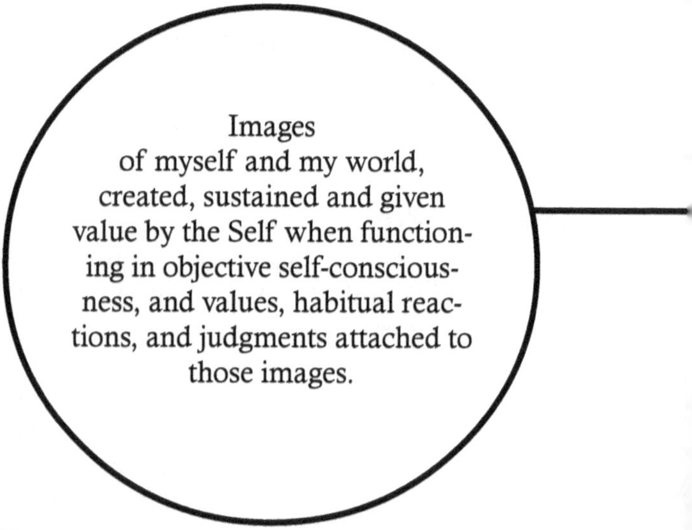

> Images of myself and my world, created, sustained and given value by the Self when functioning in objective self-consciousness, and values, habitual reactions, and judgments attached to those images.

When functioning in objective identity, we experience and express through the personality (sensation, movement, feeling, and thinking). Our attention, however, is focused almost entirely on the private world, even though the private world does not reflect or affect the real world of energy. It is nonfunctional.

The Process of Awakening 87

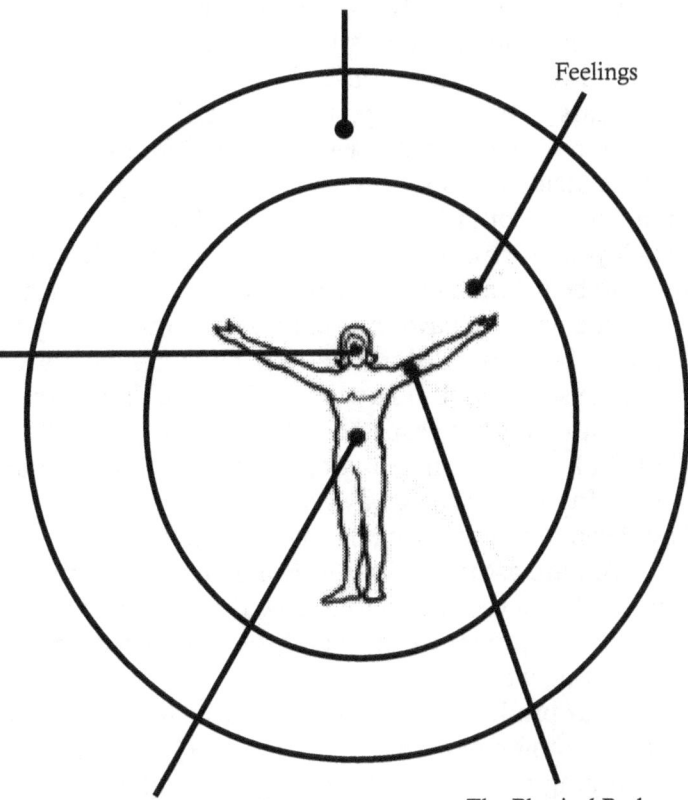

THE PERSONALITY
(functional)

Thoughts
(the objective mind)

Feelings

The Latent Power-to-Be-
Conscious at the Core or
Center of Being

The Physical Body

with you? Can't you follow the train of thought?"

Immediately you stop the inner tape recorder, which is a function of your attention, and do some quick commentary. "My brother has always hated me. He thinks I'm stupid. He wishes I were not a part of this family." You are deeply wounded by his comment and are unable to make any verbal response. This you also record in your private world.

Years go by. By now you have an archive of supportive incidents, which you have edited and inserted alongside the incident just recounted. Sometimes you use these archives to support your impoverished sense of self in which you lose track of your intelligence. Sometimes you use it to belittle and emotionally distance your brother.

One day you have the opportunity to confront your brother. You say, "I don't know why you have always hated me so much. I'm not as stupid as you think I am."

Your brother responds, "What are you talking about? I have never hated you, and I don't think you are stupid. In fact, I have always admired your intellect and have been proud that you are my brother."

You are astonished. "But I remember the time you told me I was too dumb to follow the family conversation." You recount the event as you have it recorded in your private world.

Your brother shares his memory of the same occasion. He remembers that everyone was joking around, exchanging banter, and he noticed that you were distracted. Knowing the conversation was not captivating and thinking, in his private world, that you were probably bored, he jokingly says to you, "Hey, what's the problem? Can't you follow the thread of the conversation?" He meant to imply that there wasn't any thread connecting the fragments.

You are so astonished at his private world memory of the event that you think he is making it up to make you feel better. You spend months trying to untangle the web you have woven, based on your misinterpretation of his words.

That is the nature of the private world.

Personality patterns are functional – that is, they represent our actual interactions with our environment and thus are identifiable by other persons. The private world, however, is non-functional. It represents no real interaction, or flow of energy, from one point of consciousness to another. Rather, it is a mental abstraction from and commentary on the real. No one else ever fully knows how we think and feel about our life experiences. Our *interpretations* of events remain private and personal, and to whatever degree we focus on our private worlds, to that degree we are isolated from others.

Moreover, if we live with our private worlds as our primary source of information about our lives, which most of us do, they definitely affect our personalities. We become a certain type of person – pessimistic, inspiring, wounded, helpful, etc. – because we keep a private record of our accumulated experiences that tell us who we are and what we are like. That private world life story both defines us and confines us, because it limits the way we think and feel about ourselves.

Because we are unconscious of having formed private worlds, we tend to think that our own interpretation of life is "the way it is." We not only assume the world we experience cannot be changed, but we also assume that others see and understand it the same way we do. If they seem not to, we are sure there is miscommunication rather than an actual difference in interpretations. We say, "You don't understand," as if the other *could* stand inside our private world.

When we tell others *about* our private world, they can only use their own interpretive patterns to try to understand what we are saying. They will go into their own private world looking for a way to understand ours. It cannot be done. Misunderstandings abound and the sense of isolation increases. We accuse others of not trying or not caring, but in fact it is not possible to know one another in and through our private worlds. Instead, we fall into the further trap of feeling we are "right" and others are "wrong," or vice versa.

Private worlds are not the energy world. They are a personal interpretation, and therefore distortion, of the energy world. To communicate effectively with others, we must be integrated in the dynamic flow that characterizes the energy world. The private world is like an eddy in that flow. Understanding private worlds, then – how they are formed and how they differ from the energy world – is essential for an awakening one who seeks to function with agility in the real world.

Doesn't Anyone Share Our Private Worlds?

We are certainly not isolated as we abstract images, form values, and make judgments that end up in our private worlds. We belong to groups that influence the development of our personalities and private worlds. The activities, feelings, and thoughts of other people affect us more than we realize. In fact, we create our personalities and private worlds in reaction to and/or in response to the realities of others around us. Thus it is important to become aware in a new way of the groups that have influenced us.

Usually our family groups influence us the most. We begin to notice how our taste in foods, our interests, our style of relating to others, our feelings about people who are different from us, our attitudes toward authority figures, and our educational values reflect, or are a reaction to, those of our family of origin. Then we look to see what we have adopted from our friends, from colleagues at work, from fraternal organizations, churches, racial or ethnic heritages, and our nation of origin. Each group has it own "personality" and its own private world of values, standards, preferences, and patterns of judging and reacting.

We must sort out which motivating influences and patterns we adopted from the groups with which we identify, and which we developed in reaction to those groups. This is a part of the process of freeing ourselves from the prisons of our private worlds.

For example, when I am with friends who share my love of the arts, I may assume that they will also agree with my political viewpoints and values. It is not necessarily so. In fact, I may be surprised to discover that they hold polar opposite political views. This is because, though we share identification with a group that appreciates various expressions of the arts, we are identified with completely different political groups. If I am conscious of these differences, I will not make assumptions about my friends that cause miscommunication or hurt feelings.

The same will be true in any context. Two who are attracted and fall in love based on mutual interests in several areas may discover when they marry that their family groups are radically different. Creating their own family unit with common values and rituals may prove to be a formidable task. We have to let go of the security of sharing many values and preferences with our birth family in order to create a new reality with the one we have chosen as a life partner.

Such experiences help us to recognize that, though we think of ourselves as independent, we may in fact still be very identified with various groups and those identifications may result in our virtual imprisonment in private worlds that separate us from other people we love. To function in the energy world and make choices based on individual experiences, we must free ourselves from unconscious group identifications and from unconscious adoption of the private worlds they subscribe to.

Is There Anything Positive To Say About Private Worlds?

Private worlds serve an important function in the natural order process of unfoldment, for they enable us to become conscious of ourselves as personalities. We stand apart in our private worlds, as if going into a private room in the house of Self. There we can see the world around us and ourselves in relation to it. We can evaluate what we see. We can reflect on things. We can weave our thoughts into patterns and systems of thought. Once we have established a certain amount of order in our private worlds, we can venture back into the world of interaction with the confidence that we know who we are and where we stand.

Thus the private world helps us to develop a strong sense of self. That serves us as we move forward to the next phase of our unfoldment. We know ourselves to be personalities. We understand that our personalities are expressed through our physical bodies, and that they are composed of patterns of feeling and thinking. We have grasped to a certain degree the complexity of the interaction between the facets of self. With that basis, standing in the private world of our own interpretation of who we are, we are ready for the More.

Chapter Seven

PHASE TWO OF THE AWAKENING: LEARNING TO FUNCTION CONSCIOUSLY THROUGH BODY AND PSYCHE

The second phase of awakening is in many ways the most dramatic. It is during this phase that we discover we have been asleep. We begin to distinguish between the waking dream state we have been calling real life and the awakened state of which we have been unaware. The nonreality of our private-world view of life becomes apparent the more we develop the ability to register energy consciously.

During the second phase of our awakening we expand our consciousness to discover that we are *more* than personalities. We become aware that there is a conscious control center available to us through which we can guide and direct the functional activities of the body and of the psyche. This control center we label the real Self or the spirit.

In the Wisdom traditions, it was during this second phase of the awakening process that a teacher was deemed essential. Teachers directed their students through this phase by instructing them in techniques for spiritual development. They watched to see that their students stayed grounded in their everyday lives while developing their higher faculties.

Today we are particularly blessed if we find a teacher to work with in person. If we are not so fortunate, we rely on books to point the direction and intuition to keep us on course.

How Can We Identify This Control Center In Self?

In the beginning we identify the real Self as another facet of the personality and – still identified with the personality – expand our sense of the functions of the personality to include what we label "intuition." This is a kind of knowing that is not the result of thinking, or of the abstracting process, or even of the registry of the physical senses or feelings. Intuition represents knowing that seems to go beyond our personal experience. We often say, "I don't know how I know, I just know." Or, "I just had a feeling it was so. I had no basis (meaning objective evidence) for the feeling, but I was sure it was so."

At this stage, we have broken through the shell of objective consciousness, though we may still be standing in it. We feel the presence of the energy world around us but we talk about it with words and images from life in the objective world,

Some people attempt to explain or rationalize their intuitive knowing by pointing to a source outside of self. They say, "God spoke to me," or, "I have a guide on the astral plane," or, "My inner teacher gives me guidance," or, "My departed mother comes to me and helps and directs me," or, "I have spirit guidance," or, "I hear voices," or (if the feeling response is fear), "I am possessed by evil spirits." Such reputed sources of knowing are, however, only private world abstractions: images formed in the objective mind to represent the energy reality, which are then given labels, or names. In truth, **when we register an intuition we become conscious of a new mode of functioning that belongs to a facet of Self with which we are not yet identified.** Here we label that new facet *the real Self.* Other labels for it are the Higher Self, the spirit, the Noetic Self, and Atman.

When we discover the real Self, we take a third and very important step in the individualizing process. The real Self is not a reflection of group private worlds. Instead, it is nurtured by a powerful group field called the Christos.[11] The term *the real Self* represents the emerging consciousness of a given unit or cell in the cosmic body who has awakened enough to know, "I am not just a body and I am not even just a personality or psyche; I am something much more, something that transcends time and space." When we have fully awakened, we will identify with, and know ourselves as, the real Self, and we will have developed an autonomous field of energy capable of functioning independently of all group fields except the Christos. At that point we will stand entirely free from the personal shell in which we developed.

---

[11] I use the Greek form of the word to avoid confusion for those Christians who equate the English equivalent, "the Christ," with the historical person Jesus of Nazareth. The Christos field is described in chapter nine of this book.

How Do Our Psyches Function In Reality?

Once our consciousness expands to encompass the real Self, even though we are not yet identified with it, new questions and possibilities begin to surface in our awareness. We ask ourselves, does the personality control me or do I control it? To be able to ask the question requires knowing self to be more than the personality. A new sense of "I" has awakened: "I" am not the personality, or at least not *only* the personality. We begin to allow ourselves to know that **we create our own reality**, even though we do not yet know *how* we do that.

It is to this stage of the unfolding process that much New Age literature is addressed. In an attempt to nourish the expanding sense of self, more and more persons are teaching precepts that point to our power to take charge of our own lives and to bring into being what we choose. Many of those teachings, however, fail to point out the difference between the energy world and the private world. Consequently, people attempt to create new realities by moving thought-furniture around in their private worlds. They may change the way they *think* about things, and the way they *interpret* things. But to become co-creators and to truly alter their *functional* realities, they must discover the energy world.

In fact, all that is, is energy, as the Wisdom Traditions have always taught and as modern physics has more recently established. There is no "thing" that is not composed of dynamic energy moving in patterns and configurations. With our consciousness we register the movements of the particles of energy. Their pathways are called energy waves and the rapidity of the fluctuation of the waves is called their frequency. The faster a particle moves, the more waves it creates per unit of time, and the more waves there are in a given unit of time, the shorter are the wavelengths. The term high (or fine) frequency refers to more and shorter waves in a given time unit. The term low (or gross) frequency indicates fewer and longer waves per measured unit of time.

At this stage in our awakening, it is important to adopt the language of the energy world to describe our functioning in order to free ourselves from the illusion that our images-appearing-substantive are real. *We need to align our thought processes with the way things work in the energy world.* We must also learn to distinguish between the frequencies that we register and the private world information or messages that are loaded onto those frequencies.

Let us use an analogy. A radio or television broadcasting station is assigned a wave-frequency on which to send out its programs. Each of us has a receiving set in our homes that we can tune to the designated frequency in order to enjoy those programs. The wave-frequency is always active whether or not a program is being broadcast on it (loaded on to it and carried by it). Therefore, it is possible to tune our TV or radio sets to the designated frequency, hear or see the vibration of the wave, but get no message or program if none is being sent out.

Our psyches are like broadcasting stations and receiving sets, functioning within a given spectrum of wave-frequencies. When we are broadcasting, we are sending forth messages or programs into the environment that can be picked up by other persons. When we are receiving, we tune in to given frequencies and pay attention to the programs and messages they present. It is this process of broadcasting and receiving that constitutes our functional reality.

From the functional activity of frequency registration and broadcasting, we abstract our private world realities. Until we reach this second phase of the awakening process, almost all our decisions regarding receiving and broadcasting are made unconsciously, and as a consequence, are almost entirely determined by the group fields with which we identify.

Our personal station director in charge of programming our broadcasts and of tuning the dial on our receiver set is what we are labeling the real Self. Thus, when we become conscious of the registry of frequencies in the waveband that we call the real Self, we awaken to our potential for conscious choice. Our task becomes learning to turn the "dial" of frequency registration consciously within the wavebands represented by the psyche, and to learn how to choose consciously what we will broadcast and receive.

At this stage of our awakening it is vitally important to become avid students of the Wisdom Teachings in one tradition or another. If we pay attention to our intuition, we will be guided to a teacher or a body of teachings, whether in person, through books and other published materials, or via the Internet. We are led to a presentation of the Wisdom Teachings with which we have an affinity. That vibrational resonance will nurture our emerging consciousness of the real Self. We will be able to restructure our private worlds to reflect the structure of the energy world, and equally important, we will learn how to function consciously in energy.

What follows is a foretaste of what you will learn when you engage in a serious study of the Wisdom.

What Is The Structure Of Our Human Energy Fields?

In the first stage of awakening it was helpful to identify four facets of self (body, feelings, thoughts, and intuition) and to observe with which facets we tended to identify. In this second phase of awakening it is essential to learn the structure of the individualizing Self as the Wisdom presents it. The Lower Quaternary comprises the four bodies: physical, etheric, emotional, and mental; the Higher Triad, which we are calling the real Self, reflects the essence of the primal Creative Force: will, activity, and love/wisdom. How to work consciously with this structure becomes the practical challenge of phase two.

There are five frequency wavebands in which the Lower Quaternary functions. In the Wisdom Tradition these wavebands are called chakras[12] or energy centers. The following names serve to identify the five chakras, or wavebands, of personal functioning: the Generative, the Solar Plexus, the Heart, the Throat, and the Third Eye. In other descriptions of the human energy system you will find some variation in the labels assigned, but the functional realities of the five chakras to which the names refer remain relatively constant.

While we are learning to identify these energy wavebands, it is helpful to use the body in a way analogous to a radio dial or a digital readout. When we change frequencies on a radio or TV set, we do so by mechanically turning a dial or punching a button until a marker indicates the proper frequency or a digital readout gives

---

[12] A Sanskrit word meaning "wheels."

Figure 2: THE PERSONALITY

The personality registers and expresses energy through functions (on left) associated with frequency bands of energy (on right).

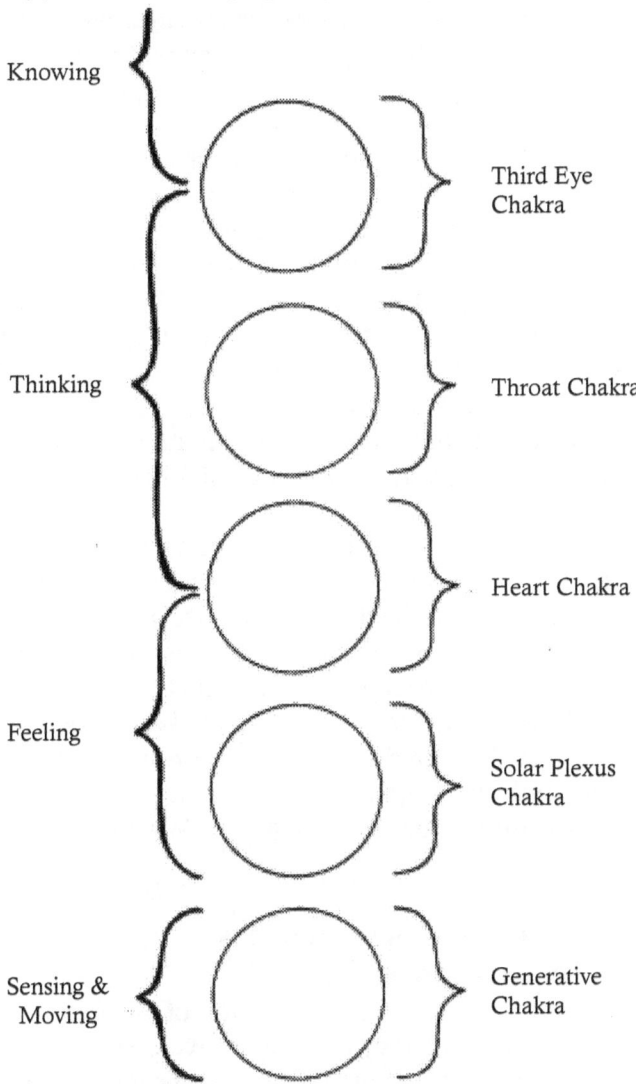

us the frequency or channel number. The actual process of identifying frequencies remains a mystery to us, but the radio and TV sets are constructed to tune in frequencies *for us* when we use the devices provided with the set.

The body can act in a similar fashion to help us tune in to chakra frequencies. If we want to register the energies of the Heart Chakra, for example, we hold our attention (which is like turning the dial or punching buttons on a remote control) on the area of the body that is associated with that frequency, namely the center of the chest. The "chest" is actually a dynamic energy system that we cannot yet see, so we use as our focus an *image* of the chest held in our psyche. Automatically and mysteriously, we will begin to register the frequencies of the Heart Center. Working with images of the body held in our psyche and with the power of our attention, we begin to discover the mysterious power of higher faculties of the mind.

Thus we can begin to identify the broad wavebands of the psyche. However, rather quickly we must teach ourselves to notice the difference between frequency registration and private world images or thoughts about such registration. We must not rely solely on the image of the body as the way to tune in to a chakra frequency. Direct registry through the extended senses is a new faculty that we will develop as we engage in the practices to which we are introduced through our Wisdom studies.

What Are The Characteristics Of The Generative Chakra?

The lowest frequency waveband of the Lower Quaternary is represented by the Generative Chakra, which is associated with the genitals and the reproductive organs of the physical body. This frequency band corresponds to energies that can be registered through the physical sense of touch and through kinesiological proprioception (sensing yourself through the muscles). The energies of the Generative Chakra are characterized by long waves pulsating slowly (relatively few waves per unit of time). They help us to establish our personal sense of time, space, and relationship (where and when we are, relative to other persons or objects).

Private world abstraction from these frequencies leads to an experience of self and others as "objects" separate from one another, acting upon and affecting one another. We think we *are* our bodies, moving in space between and among other bodies. Our movement as bodies gives us a sense of time, which is the way we measure the sensation we have as we move between one object and another. It is that sensation of duration that we call time.

Abstracted images-appearing-substantive lead to a sense that there is a world out there that is fixed and relatively stable, over which we have no control and by which our experiences are determined. Consequently, when functioning in objective identity we often feel victimized, powerless, and isolated.

If we attempt to *function* in this private world reality, we will experience nothing but frustration. Attempts to change what is out there are futile, because we are responding to images that *appear* substantive, but actually exist only in our private worlds. The only way to change those images is to change our private worlds, and we can do that only when we recognize the difference between the real energy world – the frequencies registered – and what we (and others) abstract from them and broadcast out as messages or information.

How Can We Learn To Actually Function In The Energy World?

One way to practice conscious registration of energy frequencies is to find a quiet place where you will not be interrupted. Then take a moment or two to still yourself, relaxing the body, breathing out any excess feeling energy, and inviting your mind to help you identify the difference between frequency registration and images-appearing-substantive. Focus your attention at about the level of the pelvic bone, imagining that from *inside* the body you are touching and being touched through the Generative Chakra.

As you breathe in and out, holding your attention fixed at the center of the Generative Chakra vortex or wheel, open your awareness to sounds in your environment. Discipline yourself not to form an image or give a name to any sound. Instead, pay attention to how the sound *feels* when it touches you.[13] Don't just feel it with your eardrums. Let it touch you all over your body. In fact, let go of the image of a body that the sound is touching and simply feel the sound-frequencies as they enter your energy field.

Describe the effect of the sound on your awareness with descriptive words like feathery, prickly, sharp, penetrating, soothing, quickening, constant, steady, unpredictable, flowing, thumping, pounding, etc. Or choose a

---

[13] It is helpful to realize that the five physical senses are all variations on the sense of touch. Frequency waves "touch" our consciousness as they pass through our energy fields. We have learned to identify them as touch, sound, sight, smell or taste, but in fact we register all contact in the same way: the energy wave "touches" our consciousness.

The Process of Awakening 105

simile or metaphor to help you to describe what you are registering: like gentle raindrops falling on my skin, like the touch of a feather, like being hit with pebbles, like sandpaper rubbing over the crown of my head. If you use similes and metaphors, be sure that they refer to senses other than sound: taste, touch, smell, or sight. Such "cross-sensing" helps to break up our rigid mental images so that we can identify the energy itself.

You can do a similar exercise with any of the five senses, still holding the focus of your attention at the center of the Generative Chakra (at about the level of the pelvic bone). Decide to register the frequency of scents in the air. Then discipline yourself not to form an image of what is emitting the scent or to label the scent. Instead, just experience its impact on your energy field. After a long time of being present to the experience itself, you might try to describe what the frequency is like without naming it. You might say it was all-pervasive, so sweet it seemed to stick to my field, pushing upwards and breaking through all resistance, and so forth. Let the sensation itself inform your description, not your concept or idea about the scent.

Again, if you use simile or metaphor, use something that refers to a different sensing mechanism: it was like being held in a long, close embrace on a very hot and humid day.

The most difficult sensory data to register without immediately forming an image is through the sense of sight. Images are a kind of seeing, even though the sight is inner (private world) rather than outer (energy world). Nevertheless, to distinguish the frequency of the energies we register in the waveband corresponding to sight takes long, disciplined practice. With your focus of attention still held in the Generative Chakra, allow the eyes to go slightly out of focus. This helps because it blurs the image that is forming in the psyche. Try to feel light frequencies touching your energy field. Not just your eyes, but also your entire field. Be very receptive, very yin. And discipline yourself not to form images. This practice could take you many long hours, months, and years before you finally distinguish between the registry of light frequencies and the images you associate with them.

Persist in this practice of consciously registering the frequencies of the Generative Chakra corresponding to the five senses. Eventually the sense of separation that you used to experience will fall away because you will no longer hold an image of something as the source of a sound, taste, smell, touch, or sight. In place of a feeling of separation you will be aware of living in a world of energy frequencies. You will be conscious of their constant movement through the field of your awareness. You will be immersed in the energy of sound, scent, taste, and color. You will recognize that no space separates you from them. You are one with them.

The first time the reality of this perception dawns in you, you will be thrilled to the core with the exhilaration of being alive and conscious in such a vibrant universe of energy. You will have established your own experiential referent for the term energy world.

Does This Change Our Feeling Of Separation From The World Around Us?

Caught in objective self-consciousness where we see ourselves as irrevocably separate from other persons, we often attempt to change our private world realities of loneliness and isolation by engaging in sexual intercourse with someone – the nearest physical representation of union available to us. But separation always follows the union. There is no way by activity (a Generative Chakra functional expression) to change the private world reality, or belief, that we are separated and out of union.

We can only change the experience of loneliness and isolation by shifting our consciousness to the functional reality of the dynamic energy world. When we learn to register energy directly and consciously, we discover that we are already integrated in, one with, and inseparable from the Whole. In that state of consciousness we realize there is nothing we need to change to eradicate loneliness and isolation except our state of consciousness. We need only to be conscious of, and function in, what already is.

What Can We Broadcast On the Frequencies Of the Generative Chakra?

The **Love Principle**[14] *Be the Change You Want to See Happen*, rather than trying to change anyone (or everyone) else, is a reminder to shift out of the private world into functional reality. To **be some change** we have to embody it, become it. We do this through the energies of the Generative Chakra, setting activity in motion through our own vehicle of change, the body. This **Love Principle** invites us to pay attention to frequencies registered in this and other chakras. What we register often arouses the desire for change. In response to that desire, we can make

---

[14] The Love Principles are a practical approach to opening the Heart Center in Universal Love and harmonizing the energies of the other chakras with that Love. See *The Love Principles* by Arleen Lorrance, Scottsdale, AZ: Teleos Imprint, 2002.

conscious choices about what to broadcast or send forth as our response.

What Are The Characteristics Of The Solar Plexus Chakra?

The next higher frequency band registered in the psyche, representing a higher number of waves per unit of measured time and shorter wave lengths, is labeled the Solar Plexus Chakra. In the body, the Solar Plexus corresponds to the digestive organs, with the bowels representing the core. These are energy frequencies that enable us to sense the relational impact of one center of consciousness on another. Put in the simplest terms, when we register Solar Plexus Center energy frequencies, we are either moved to expand toward the one broadcasting or to contract in their presence. We are attracted or repelled according to our registry of a pleasurable sensation or a painful one, in much the same way as we find food either to our taste or not.

We have more difficulty, as a general rule, digesting experiences that are very painful. It is not unusual for people who experience something horrible to vomit, as if seeking to expel from their energy fields the vibratory food they ingested. And it may be weeks, months, or years before such persons process the experience by feeling all the feelings they called up in response. Figures of speech such as, "what a distasteful experience that was," or "I can't stomach him," or "she makes me sick to my stomach" reflect the close association between Solar Plexus registry and the digestive organs.

The private world data abstracted from the wave frequencies of the Solar Plexus Chakra are given feeling-labels. On the pain side: loneliness, hurt, suffering, grief, fear, dislike, hate, envy, jealousy, greed, anger, etc. On the pleasure side: delight, excitement, peace, contentment, satisfaction, fondness, love, happiness, fun, enjoyment, etc. When private world values are attributed to polar opposite experiences, painful feelings are often judged to be bad and pleasureful experiences good. Without knowing how to work with the energy centers on the conscious level, people often close down the Solar Plexus Chakra in order to avoid unpleasant experiences.

However, the shutdown of the chakra in such a case comes only *after* a feeling is formed. Rather than avoid the painful experience, we actually prolong it, for functionally we have no way of releasing the energy once the chakra is closed. Moreover, in the moment of judging that this was a bad experience, we have incorporated the pain into the private world where we suffer an *awareness* of it but cannot change it, because the private world is completely nonfunctional in relation to the energy world.

When we are still (to whatever degree) functioning in a state of objective self-consciousness, we almost inevitably perceive that someone or something else "made" us feel the way we feel. In our private worlds we attribute blame and fault, and we feel powerless to change what we are experiencing. We feel dependent on some "other" to make us feel better. Once again we are trapped in our private worlds where we cannot bring about any change.

In the energy world we are trapped only by our ignorance of the way the chakras function. When we learn, we will be able to direct the energy and create something different.

How Can We Move Into The Energy World In The Solar Plexus Chakra?

Our first challenge, as was the case with the Generative Chakra, is to learn to tell the difference between the frequencies registered and our private world interpretation of them. Begin by adopting the premise that how you feel is not determined by anything outside yourself. At first this will be difficult, because the habit of blaming others for how we feel is very well established. Experiment with the premise that you *choose* a feeling response to what you register from someone or something else.

Here is an example to illustrate the new premise. Three people are playing on a softball team and are about to go up to bat. The coach shouts in a very loud voice, "Hit the g-damned ball!"

Player #1 hears the words and goes directly to her private world. "I wish he wouldn't swear at me," she thinks. She feels emotionally wounded and morally offended. By the time she gets to the plate she wishes she were not on this team playing for this coach. She does not *want* to hit the ball, and she doesn't. Her private world has won the inner game, but she blames her failure to hit the ball on her coach.

Player #2 hears the words and goes directly to his private world. "He has confidence in me. He believes I can hit the ball. I hope I don't let him down. What if I miss? Will he be disappointed in me?" He swings and misses, three times. He is not as concerned about losing the game as he is about disappointing his coach.

Player #3 experiences the words as they hit her energy field. She doesn't go to her private world at all. If you asked her later she would tell you she doesn't know what the coach said. What she *feels* is a tremendous rush of energy, as if someone had just given her a direct shot of adrenalin. She feels suddenly more alive and more alert. She steps to the plate and meets the ball with tremendous force. As she watches the ball head out to center field she feels a second rush of energy. She flies off homebase and heads for first as if she were a canon ball released with a blast of dynamite. As she approaches first base she sees the first base coach waving her on. She doesn't hesitate. It is as though the movement of his arms gives her a shove and she is off and running to second base. She stops there. The opposing team throws the ball to third base. Only then does she go to her private world. "Wow! What a rush! I did it!" She considers her double to be an exciting event in which she had the privilege to participate. She responded in the energy world instead of separating herself from it by interpreting and attributing blame or taking credit.

To learn to function consciously through the Solar Plexus, you must suspend all labeling of the energy that comes to you from others. Moreover, don't step back to try to determine the motive of the one who spoke or acted. Instead, focus your attention at the naval, but inside your body, and experience the energy that comes to you. *Feel* it, don't label it. See what it awakens in you energetically. Do you, for example, feel quickened, stimulated, energized, or evoked? Or do you feel flattened, weighted down, burdened, or crushed? Without placing any attention on the one from whom the energy came, determine what you want to do in response. If you can stay out of your private world, you will surprise yourself with your response.

There are two keys here to functioning in the energy world. Ask yourself, **How does the energy I am registering**

feel, *and what do I* **want to do** *in response?* Imagine how many adults would avoid abusive relationships if they functioned this way. The first time a partner did or said something that felt painful, they would ask, "What do I want to do in response?" The majority would respond, "Get out!" And if they didn't go into their private worlds to try to understand *why* partners did what they did or said what they said, or to make *excuses* for them, or to take the *blame* onto themselves, they would simply get out! That would be the natural order response and would avoid long years of suffering to prove to their private worlds that their first impulse was the correct one.

Or perhaps they would not immediately get out. Perhaps instead they would say, "If you do or say that again, I am out of here." In that way they would respond to their energetic registry and leave the door open for the partner to change. But there would be no doubt in them that they would not want to continue to subject themselves to such gratuitous pain.

The same would be true with work environments. If we allowed ourselves to register in the Solar Plexus our feeling response to our work environment and to ask, "What do I want to do in response?" we would find it easier to move on from work that would eventually make us sick if we stayed.

Things are simple in the energy world. They are direct and uncomplicated. Lines are clear. Change can occur in an instant. And the change can be reversed in an instant. The key is to trust our registry in the Solar Plexus and to ask ourselves, what do I want in response?

Can We Always Have What We Want?

Sometimes we choose to endure solar plexus pain for a higher purpose. For example, we may find having dental work done is not pleasant, yet we choose it because we are aware that letting our teeth rot will, in the long run, bring more pain. Or, we may *want* to have an alcoholic drink, but our past experience tells us that if we have one we will not be able to stop, so we deny ourselves the apparent pleasure of one drink to prevent the disaster we know will follow. Or, outer circumstances may deny us what we want in a given situation. For example, we may want to date someone but he/she doesn't want to date us, or we may want to go out for the evening but our parents won't let us. In these and other situations we may not get what we want, at least not immediately.

However, being aware of what we want does make the choice-making clear and easy. For example, if I know that I do not want to go to the dentist, then I will be motivated to take better care of my teeth. If I know that I want to have an alcoholic drink, then I will know that it is still important for me to go to my AA meetings regularly. If I want to date someone for the pleasure of his/her company, then I know that I do *not* want to go out with him/her if the feeling is not mutual. But I *do* want to find someone else who will reciprocate my attraction. And if I want to go out for the evening but my parents won't let me, then I know I want to find out what I need to do to earn my parents' trust.

When we really get into trouble is when we don't let ourselves *know* what we want. Then we are unable to evaluate and unable to make decisions for ourselves.

How Will We Determine Whether To Pursue What We Want Or To Set Preferences Aside?

The **Love Principle** *Problems Are Opportunities* is a reminder not to pass judgment on the feelings we register and not to attempt to block out pain-evoking interactions.

Feeling responses, whether of pleasure or pain, provide opportunities to become conscious of the impact of different energy-expressions on our consciousness. Only by consciously *registering* these Solar Plexus frequencies can we respond to the opportunities they represent for new understanding, growth, change, learning, and action.

Feelings give us information about our experiences. How we respond to that information is our own choice when we are conscious. If we are not conscious we automatically go into the private world and begin labeling, judging, rationalizing, and reacting. We can learn to determine whether the energy we register *requires* a response from us or not. Sometimes we will register enormous pain and be aware that it is not ours to deal with. In those moments we might choose to transmute the pain by raising it into our heart centers. But that takes us to a next level of understanding of how to work with conscious registry in the chakras and conscious expression through them.

What Are The Characteristics Of The Heart Chakra?

We label the next higher waveband of energy frequencies in which the psyche functions the Heart Center. These frequencies represent an opportunity for the personality to experience the perfect equilibrium, balance, peace, harmony, and joy that can be ours when we learn to respond to directives from the real Self. These frequencies are characterized by more waves per unit of measured time and shorter wave lengths than Solar Plexus energies, and represent the mid-point, or balance-point, in the range of personal expression and experience, the point of perfect stability and security.

When private world interpretations or abstractions are made from Heart Center frequencies registered, they tend to be colored by either feelings or thoughts. Thus, when identified with feelings, we might label the experience of Heart Center frequencies as pity, sympathy, compassion, and/or a desire to help. When identified with the objective mind, we might label the experience of the same frequencies as empathetic understanding, benevolent judgment, and/or soft-heartedness that could lead to a failure to exercise good judgment.

Heart Center frequencies themselves, when not carrying feeling- or thought-prompted messages, are actually quite neutral. They are not characterized by either feeling or logic. Rather, they provide a state of functional equilibrium within which conscious choices can easily be made. It is in the Heart Center that we first experience how much more eclectic, tolerant, and universal we become when we are liberated from the restricting perspective of our private worlds. From the more encompassing view of life as energy, we can dip into our private worlds for value assessments and decision making without getting stuck there. We can also invite others to give us their private world opinions and assessments, using them to expand our own seeing. In other words, the Heart Center energies provide easy access to the energy world.

As long as we remain identified with the personality, it is difficult to register Heart Center energy frequencies without a private world interpretation, and thus distortion. However, the **Love Principle** *Receive all People as Beautiful Exactly As They Are* is a reminder that it is possible to let the Life Force quicken our fields without qualification (without any private world data being communicated or abstracted), and to share that quickening with all with whom we come into contact, in every here/now moment.

When on a rare occasion we do register Heart Center frequencies without private world interference, we experience an exhilarating union with the All (the whole universe) or a given "other" (a tree, a flower, a person). So profound and total is the experience of union that it is often unsettling if we are still identified with the personality. The temptation is to ask, "What does it mean?" and to withdraw to the private world to seek an answer. In the functional energy reality there *is* no meaning, in the abstract sense of that word, to an experience of union. It simply is.

To seek for a meaning, an interpretation, in the private world, is to ask objective consciousness to account for a union that never occurred on the objective level. This can lead to much confusion. We might be tempted to make the union happen objectively, in order to bring the two realities – the functional energy world experience and the private world abstraction from it – into alignment. We might seek to marry the person, to have sexual intercourse with him/her, or to share a life and work with him/her. If the union was not with a person, but rather with something else (a tree, flower, etc.) or the All, we might interpret the experience as a special calling to a mystical life, to do spiritual work, to enter the ministry, or to withdraw from the material world.

In life fact – that is to say, on the functional energy level – the union experienced when we register Heart Center frequencies is "the way it is" in the energy world. What we register is our integral oneness with the Whole, our union with all who are and all that is. On the one hand, there is nothing to be done about that reality, for it simply is. On the other hand, *everything* we do, feel, think, and say will be altered when we fully realize that we are intimately connected with, interwoven in the fabric of life with, everyone and everything. Our personalities become life-long expressions of Universal and Unconditional Love, the force that links and binds all facets and aspects of energy-in-manifestation into one unified Whole. We become instruments of living love, expressing through our personalities only that which enhances the well being of all life expressions.

How Can We Learn To Function Through The Heart Chakra In The Energy World?

The best way I know to practice the registry of Heart Center frequencies is to breathe deeply, in and out, with a focus on the center of the chest between the lungs. By consciously breathing in and out, you are circulating cosmic energy, in much the same way the heart and lungs circulate life-giving energy in your physical body. Whenever you breathe in air on the physical level, you are also breathing in higher frequency energy even if you are not aware of it. The air feeds the physical body, carrying oxygen to the blood, which then circulates it to all the cells. The higher frequency energies feed the more subtle levels of your energy field of which you will become conscious as your consciousness of self continues to expand. In this natural way, consciously breathing in and breathing out, you can train your awareness to work with the realm of the unseen — the Life Force, the universe, the cosmos, God. You ground that cosmic force every time you breathe, making the unseen Life Force flesh.

Concentrate on staying open to everything and everyone, as if you had a revolving door in the center of your chest and you were allowing everything in your life to pass through your awareness without any obstruction or interpretation or judgment. Stay out of your private world. Don't think about these energetic exchanges. Just invite them and experience them. Your life will be enormously enriched as a result. Heart Center love is like the energy of the sun: it is shared indiscriminately with all.

In time we become aware that there is a different faculty of seeing and knowing that opens in the Heart Center. It is the perception of beauty, a beauty so vivid and life giving that it often evokes tears of gratitude in response. Perhaps the most familiar experience of this kind of seeing is reflected in our response to infants. Almost universally we exclaim, "Oh, what a beautiful child," as if we recognize the presence of the One, of God, in this new life. We smile and feel full of love, welcoming the little one into our world with our energy embrace. We do not mean that the child is beautiful physically. We are responding to the vibrant Life Force that is present in the infant.

To see the beauty in all that is has nothing to do with esthetic appreciation. It is also not an expression of what you like or are attracted to. Rather, the heart senses the universal Life Force Itself in and through each and every person and object, and the heart melts into a pool of passionate praise and thanksgiving for the privilege of being alive in the presence of such beauty.

How Can We Characterize The Throat Chakra?

The next higher waveband of energy frequencies registered in the psyche is labeled the Throat Chakra. This energy center is characterized by wave frequencies higher (shorter in length and more waves per unit of measured time) than those of the Heart Center. The frequencies of the Throat Chakra are the frequency regulators for the energy world in which the personality functions. To register and transmit these energies consciously is to gain conscious control over the functions of the psyche. These frequencies represent our mental activities.

The Throat Chakra energies have the power to resonate the energies of other chakras by harmonizing with them frequency to frequency, thus setting the other energy waves in motion, or vibrating them. Thus by speaking, someone can incite others to action, evoke certain feelings in them, cause them to think certain thoughts or to gain certain insights, and even to form given images in their consciousness. Great orators have mastered the use of Throat Chakra energies; their words deeply affect all who hear them. Great leaders usually have the same mastery. But *anyone* who has begun to learn how to utilize the Throat Chakra energies consciously has experienced the feeling of power that comes when, by thinking, speaking, or writing, we are able to influence the thoughts, words, and actions of others.

By activating Throat Chakra frequencies, we can similarly awaken the energy of other chakras in our own energy fields. If we think or speak about past experiences, convictions we hold, persons in our lives, etc., we may stir our own feelings, cause our own tears to flow, release a flood of images and thoughts, and/or come to see something new and understand something more deeply than we did before.

Moreover, it is possible to channel and release the energy of other chakras by giving form and expression to them through the Throat Center, in thought, written, or spoken words. When an impulse to embrace someone surges in the Generative Chakra, but it is inappropriate to embody the impulse with that person or in the given circumstances, the energy can be lifted into the Throat Chakra. We might say, "I could just hug you for saying that." When we give the energy expression through words, we gain conscious control over the impulse and are able to release it through the words.

Or suppose you are registering complete hopelessness and despair in the Solar Plexus and you are afraid you will express the energy through destructive actions in Generative Chakra frequencies. An alternative is to lift the despair into the Throat Chakra waveband where you can express it in powerful words and verbally described images. Not only will your words give form to your feelings, but they will also help others to express and release their despair. Great poets have utilized this power of the written and spoken word for millennia, and their words provide generations of humans with vehicles to channel the energy of unexpressed thoughts, feelings, and impulses to action that would otherwise go unexpressed.

The power of Throat Center energies to exercise control over other frequencies is proportionate to the degree of consciousness of the person activating the Throat Chakra. If we are relatively unconscious, we can do a great deal of thinking and speaking without having much effect on others or on ourselves. The more conscious we become, however, the more what we think and say evokes resonating energy in others and/or in our own being. When we learn to function in total consciousness, we will be able simply to speak and it will be so. The words will take form in the energy world in frequencies that even the neurological system of ordinary humans can register.

Do We Use Throat Chakra Energies To Form Our Private Worlds?

The Throat Chakra is our port of entry to private worlds. The process of abstracting which eventuates in the private world is loaded onto Throat Chakra energy waves. Therefore, to gain conscious access to our own private worlds and to share them with others, we activate Throat Chakra energies and become aware of the private world messages carried by them.

Many forms of meditation help us to develop the ability to observe the activities of Throat Chakra frequencies. By placing our attention at the level of the Adam's apple, encompassing the area of the body from the shoulders up to and including the vocal chords, the ears, the jaw and mouth, we can begin to recognize the frequencies that correspond to this chakra. In addition, we can observe the thoughts and images that are being carried on those frequencies. Meditation teachers will often say, "Watch your thoughts as they pass through." As we do, we become aware that we live in a sea of thoughts and that we can choose consciously which ones to register and contemplate and which ones to let pass on by without lending our energy to them.

Our private worlds are like eddies in that large sea of thoughts. Moving contrary to the main flow, circling back to think about what is past, they have almost no effect on the sea itself, but they can distort our perceptions to such a degree that we cannot see what is beyond the eddy. Meditation helps us to gain a larger view and to detach from the whirling movement of the private world.

Don't Words Also Provide Bridges To Other People?

The **Love Principle** *Provide Others With Opportunities To Give* is a reminder that we can have conscious control over whether or not we will open ourselves to others and allow them to contribute to our lives, to what extent, when and how. Each of us can learn to be the gatekeeper of our own energy field, consciously choosing what frequencies we will register and what messages we will send out in response.

It is also by making our wants and needs known that we invite others to give to us, and we can most easily and directly do that by putting them into words. Thus we take responsibility in the Throat Chakra for two primary aspects of the give and take between people. First, we are direct about our communications with loved ones (and also with strangers, when appropriate) so that they do not have to engage in guessing games to discover how to please us. And second, we acknowledge through asking and receiving that we know we are not alone in the world. We need others. And we are enriched by what others give to us.

Why Is The Next Energy Center Called The "Third" Eye Chakra?

The fifth of the energy centers corresponding to the psyche is called the Third Eye Chakra. There are not "three eyes," or three different levels of reality, or three bands of frequency corresponding to one level of reality. Rather, *the three eyes represent different phases in the develop-*

ment of our physiological organism's ability to transmit via its nervous system the light frequencies we register in our consciousness. For example, at the level of development that the "first eye" represents – what is called physical sight – the nerves are unable to transmit the interstices between rapid impulses of light frequency registration. Instead, the impulses blur together so that what we "see" with our consciousness is the general outline of the object of our perception – a gestalt of the light rays reflected by the energy configuration being perceived. Thus to our objective consciousness things look solid, separate from one another, and fixed in time and space.

When the nerves develop sufficiently to transmit a higher frequency of light energy waves, we say our second, or psychic, eye opens. At this stage in our development, our nerves are still blurring the impulses and we continue to be aware of gestalts, or images. But through the psychic eye, forms are perceived as less solid and are often described as diaphanous. Moreover, separate spaces appear less clearly defined, so that objects or things are often seen to pass through one another. Events seem less fixed in time and space, and thus appear to encompass a larger spectrum of the time/space continuum. Consequently, psychic events are often described as "out of the past' or "in the future" and/or in locations distant to the space seemingly occupied by the perceiver.

What actually happens when the second eye opens is that our seemingly solid objective reality begins to take on a dream-like quality. It does not seem so objectively real anymore. Though we tend to respond to psychic perception with the same private world process of interpretation and value judgment as we do with physical perception, we begin to question the nature of reality in general and to give more credence to subjective experiences than we did in earlier phases. This prepares us to perceive the energy world as it is.

When the nervous system of the human being is still more fully developed or refined, it is able to transmit registered impulses much more rapidly, and we are able to see energy directly. The Third Eye symbolizes the registry of energy frequencies with interstices between wave impulses still intact. Gestalts, or images, give way to aggregations of energy units that appear to have identifiable textures or qualities due to lines of force that form distinctive energy patterns. All appearance of separate spaces gives way to the perception of one cohesive field with identifiable or recognizable fields within fields within the overall field. The perception of time/space yields to a sense of an all-pervasive now, which encompasses all that ever was, is and will be. The perception represented by the Third Eye is spherical, as though from a center point outward or inward in every direction at once.

So Is This Chakra About Literal Seeing?

This is the band of wave frequencies representing our awareness, or perception, in a much broader sense than just literal seeing. The registry of Third Eye Chakra frequencies also encompasses understanding. Data taken in is organized or reorganized on Throat Chakra frequencies until it falls into a coherent pattern that makes sense. When this happens, we register the new pattern in the Third Eye Chakra and say, "I see!" That seeing represents conscious understanding of the information, or recognition of a larger pattern into which the data fit.

Insights are also registered in the Third Eye Chakra. These are perceptions of a different order. It is as if we are able to rearrange the particles of previous perception until they fall together into a new pattern. The new pattern, seen within, gives us the ability to recognize and understand some aspect of the energy world more clearly, or perhaps just differently.

How Can We Function More Consciously Through The Third Eye Center?

The **Love Principle** *Create Your Own Reality Consciously* is an invitation to see the dynamic energy world *as it is* without being limited to private world abstractions. You can begin to practice by learning to tell the difference between the energy world and the private world. When you have an experience, describe what happened without any interpretation.

For example, "I walked into the store at about 9:15 AM. My boss Helen was already at work restocking the shelves. She turned to face me. Her face turned red. She began to shout. I could not understand all of her words. She turned and went into the stock room, slamming the door behind her."

Then record, separately, your private world commentary on what happened: "I was embarrassed to be arriving fifteen minutes late, but I had a good excuse. Helen seemed furious at me. She never gave me a chance to speak. She was practically incoherent she was so angry. I couldn't imagine how fifteen minutes could make so much difference. I felt battered and hurt. When she stomped out of the room, I thought she was being very childish."

As you practice separating out the simple facts of an event from your thoughts about it, your assessments and judgments, you will begin to realize that much of your private world commentary is speculation rather than fact. It has a greater influence over your response than the actual events do.

In this way, you will practice being conscious of how you *create your reality* in your private world. Then you can practice taking a second step, namely, making a conscious choice about how to respond.

In the above example, you might choose not to take Helen's outburst personally. You might go to the door of the stock room and knock quietly, asking for permission to enter. If Helen grants it, you might say something like, "May we talk for a minute?" With each response Helen makes, you can make a conscious choice about how to proceed. She might say, "We have nothing to talk about. You are fired."

Since you have no more information than that she doesn't think/feel you have anything to talk about and she has fired you, you might choose to stay open to her instead of getting defensive and angry, or giving up. You might say, "May I ask why?" Or, you might say, "I understand that you do not want to talk with me and that you have fired me. May I say a few words?" If she is willing to hear you out, you might say, "I wanted to apologize for being late this morning and explain what happened that caused me to be late." If she is still listening, you could give your explanation and then wait for her response.

If Helen does not want to listen to what you have to say, you might say, "Would you like me to work out the day so that you are not left without help?" If she agrees, you could hope she might cool off so that you could talk later.

The point is that you can make conscious choices about what reality you want to create as you move through an interaction *if you know the difference between your private world and the energy world.* Your private world will continue to run its commentary, but you do not have to let that determine your response. If it says, "What an idiot she is!" you can respond internally with "thank you for your opinion" or "that's not helpful right now." You can take charge of both your internal (private world) conversation and your responses in the external (energy world) interaction.

The principle *create your own reality consciously* is an invitation to identify with the real Self in order to activate the flow of force which alone can release true creativity – namely, that which is registered in, and channeled and directed by, the real Self. It helps to see that we have created our reality (the nature of our experience) by abstracting images and then attributing values to them. As my teacher used to say, "Nothing can affect us except the value we attribute to it." In the example given above, if I have a high value on being polite, then I might judge that Helen was very rude to shout at me. In the judgment, I narrow my options for how to respond to her. If I value plain talk even when it doesn't feel good, I will be able to stay more open to Helen after she shouts at me. Helen doesn't change. I change according to the value I put on her response to me.

Later in the interaction I may have a very high value on keeping this job. If so, I will probably feel very threatened by her words "you are fired." I will feel I am in jeopardy because I value the job and the income it gives me. If I value my relationship with Helen, I may be more threatened by her anger than by the fact that she has just fired me. If I really don't put much value on this job or my relationship with Helen, then neither her anger nor her words "you are fired" will affect me very much.

It may be helpful to make a list of your values. List values under several headings: what you value in relationships, in the arts, in recreation, in your home life, in your past, in your work life, in your spiritual life, etc. Then go back over the list to discover, if you can, where you got that value. Does it reflect a group you belong to, an influential person in your life, an experience you once had, etc.

Then ask yourself whether you want to continue to hold each of the values you have listed. Begin to prioritize values. Put at the top, those you would never compromise if you could help it. Put farther down the list those that are preferences, but could fall away if a higher value was at stake.

Once you have looked at your values in this way, you will find that it is easier to make conscious choices for yourself. For example, if you value your independence and loving companionship about equally, you may find it easier to say yes to shared activities about half the time and yes to going your own way the other half. But if you value your independence above all, then you may discover that your friendships suffer as a result. You need to be sure that your value on companionship is not very high or you will not be happy.

When you are clear about your own values, you will also find it easier not to judge others. You may value contributing to organizations that help people who are homeless. If your friend doesn't want to contribute to the same organizations, it may be that he values making his own way in life through hard work. His decision not to contribute reflects what he values as much as your decision does. The values are different, not right or wrong.

When we begin to recognize that values are arbitrary, not absolute, we can suspend our automatic judgments and turn to the real Self for a different point of view. The real Self sees with a comprehensive overview that leads not only to understanding but also to compassion. It sheds Light on our inner process of reality creation and in so doing illumines the personality and radiates through it to other persons. The more we are aware of this Light, the easier it becomes to realize that we *are* the real Self.

You might also want to experiment with consciously broadcasting messages on Third Eye Center frequencies. Hold a thought in your awareness. Then, visualize sending that thought out on a beam of light through your forehead to another person. Whenever it occurs to you, beam it out again. Then wait to see if you get a confirmation that the person received your thought. You might start with something simple, like, "Call me." The person might not call, but they might tell you later, "I kept meaning to call but didn't" or "I kept thinking about you all day yesterday."

In these and other practices, you will begin to recognize how you *create your own reality* and how you might do so more *consciously.*

What Else Do We Learn About Our Psyches During This Phase Of The Awakening?

There are two more vitally important things we learn about our psyches. The first is that psyches function entirely by **reflection**. The astral energy of which they are composed acts as a kind of mirror. Whatever the psyche is exposed to, it reflects back in feeling and thought. The etheric body then transmits the reflection to the physical body, which gives it form and expression.

130 AWAKENING TO WISDOM

Figure 3: THE PERSONALITY

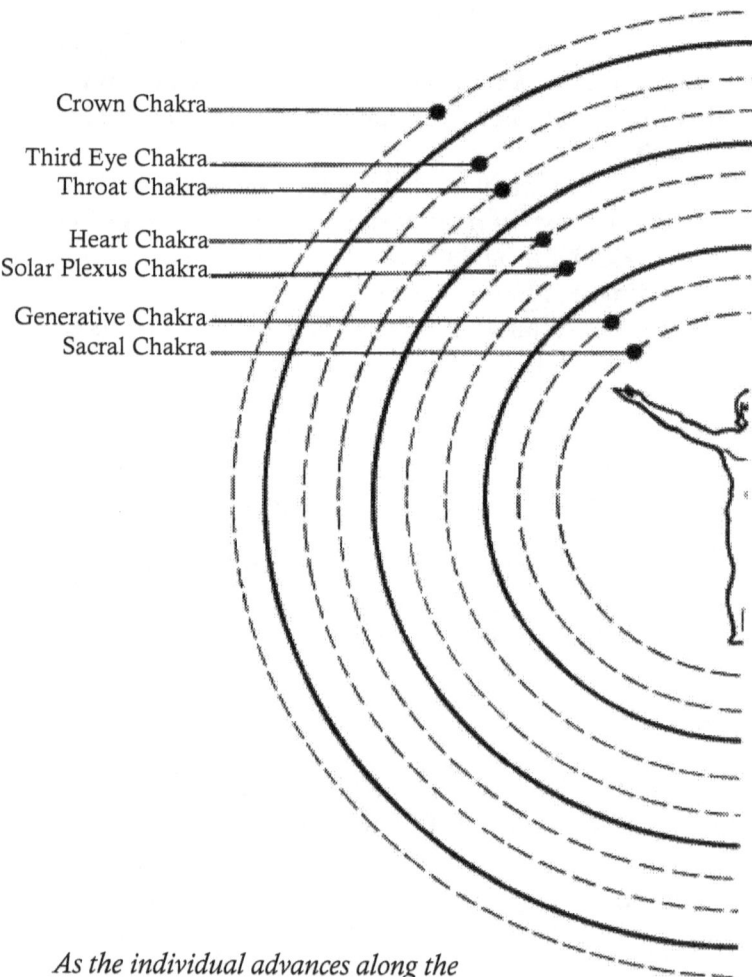

- Crown Chakra
- Third Eye Chakra
- Throat Chakra
- Heart Chakra
- Solar Plexus Chakra
- Generative Chakra
- Sacral Chakra

As the individual advances along the path toward wholeness, the chakras and the faculties for registering and expressing energy become synthesized into an integral whole.

IN EXPANDED AWARENESS

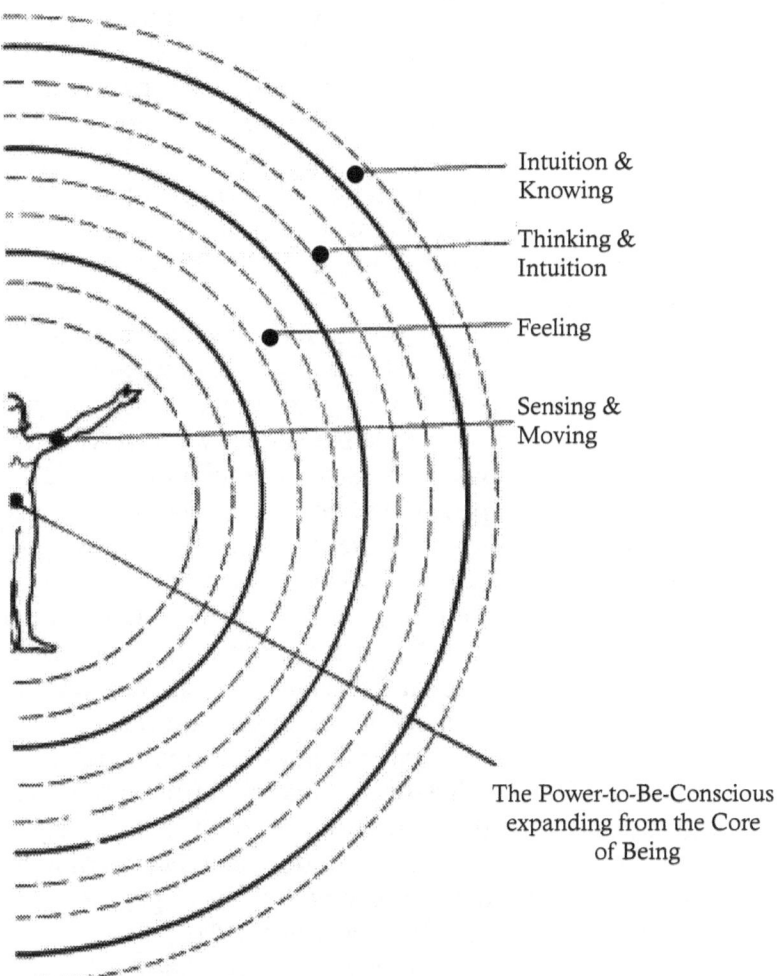

- Intuition & Knowing
- Thinking & Intuition
- Feeling
- Sensing & Moving

The Power-to-Be-Conscious expanding from the Core of Being

This explains why children who are raised in abusive families become abusers themselves. Their psyches have been deeply impressed with the attitudes, words and behavior to which they were exposed as children. When they become adults, they simply reflect back what was first imprinted on them. I remember a young friend of mine reporting, in genuine despair, that she had "become" her mother. She said she would open her mouth to speak to her children and hear her own mother shouting abusively at her. Only the expressions on her children's faces made her realize that she herself was doing the shouting.

The example of a psyche reflecting abusive parents is dramatic, but in fact all of us, as long as we are unconscious, are merely mirroring what we have been exposed to. There has been much debate about whether violence depicted on television breeds violence in the children who watch it. If people understood the laws that govern our psyches they would realize that not only children, but also adults are imprinted by what they watch.

As we become more conscious, we are able to filter what we are exposed to so that we don't automatically reflect it back in our own thoughts, feelings, and actions. But even then we will often find images appearing in our nighttime dreams that we thought we had not allowed to affect us. Our psyches work diligently through the night to sort out what they have been exposed to. By bringing our nighttime dreams into consciousness upon waking, we get a clearer picture of how much our psyches have picked up from our experiences of the day past.

We have to learn to work with this knowledge. *The only way we can change how we think, how we feel, and even how we act, is to impress the psyche with images of what we wish to manifest.* We must carefully select what we read and watch, the people we associate with, the thoughts we entertain, the music we listen to, etc., making sure that they represent the qualities and characteristics we wish to embody. And when we are trying to change patterns, we need to recognize that the exposure to the new images needs to be as long and powerful as were the images we seek to replace. Long repetition of the new is necessary before the old begins to fade out.

When I first began to study the Wisdom, I recognized that I could not understand most of it because it contradicted much that I had been taught in the Church. So I decided to saturate my psyche with the new information. I bought tapes of Vitvan's lesson series. All day long, while I was doing housework, preparing meals, exercising, or doing office work that did not require much attention, I wore earphones and played the lesson series over and over again. Seven years later, I began to feel I could grasp the Teachings when I read them. In my early years my psyche was saturated with the teachings of the Church; now it was equally saturated with the Wisdom Teachings. Until then, my psyche could not help me to manifest the Teachings.

The other law governing the psyche is **suggestion**. By suggestion I mean that we let the psyche know what we want by *holding clear images*. Then we let go, trusting the psyche to manifest what we want rather than trying to tell it how to do it. We do not direct the psyche's process after we make clear what we want.

The psyche is very responsive to suggestion. As a result, you could be reading inspirational material, keeping company with high-minded people, and setting conscious intentions for your life. But if you have an image of yourself as someone who could never live that way or who is not strong enough to stay with the program, your psyche will pick up on the suggestion and all the active things you are doing will be wasted.

On the other hand, if your life seems to be a mess and you don't see how to straighten things out, but you feel strongly that you are learning a lot, your psyche will pick up your suggestion and will manifest that. Later you may say, "I can't believe what I went through last year, but you know, I feel more solid in myself than I ever have before because *I learned so much*," forgetting that you were the one who planted that suggestion in your psyche.

It is because the psyche is so quick to pick up indirect suggestions that we should not worry about the outcome of things, or harbor fears. We are deluged with images these days, especially on television, in movies, on the Internet, and in video games. Those images are giving suggestions to our psyches. Sometimes the psyche will pick up the suggestion and motivate the individual to *embody* the image. Hence, we have heinous acts of cruelty and murder committed by children and teenagers who lead otherwise normal lives. Sometimes the psyche recycles the images as if predicting what will happen in the future. These images can evoke great anxiety and fear. If we harbor those fearful images and support them with powerful feelings about what could happen, sooner or later your worst fears will be realized. If, on the other hand, you hold a clear image of what you *want* to have manifest in your life, what you envision will eventually come into being, often in ways you could not have imagined.

When the psyche picks up suggestion, it works in cooperation with other forces in subconsciousness to manifest what is wanted or needed. I remember one time when I was several hundred dollars short of what I needed to pay for a new typewriter. I had visualized myself owning the typewriter, and I had registered clearly the dollar amount and the date it was due. Then I did not think about it any more, but simply went about living my life. Shortly before the typewriter was to be delivered, a check came in the mail from a friend I hadn't heard from for several years. She said she wanted to repay the money I had loaned her about eight years earlier. I had completely forgotten about the loan and I certainly had not told her that I needed the money now. But somehow my psyche worked it out with hers, and the check for almost the exact amount needed came in the mail just in time to meet my deadline.

I have had many examples of the workings of the psyche in this way. Very often when I am driving to an event and I know the parking lot will be crowded, I visualize an empty parking space near the entrance. If I give my psyche sufficient notice, it almost never fails to "produce" the parking space. I remember a time when I was meeting a friend for lunch at a busy restaurant. He also requests parking places. When I arrived, my space was waiting for me right in front of the restaurant. Tom was several minutes late meeting me. When he arrived he said, "You took my parking place! As I was arriving, you were backing into *my* space." We both laughed, because neither of us had thought to ask for two spaces in front of the restaurant!

Learning to work with the laws of reflection and suggestion as they work in the psyche is a major part of the work of phase two of the process of awakening. This work cannot be done in the private world; it must be done in the dynamic energy world. We cannot just *think* about it; we must learn how to use our creative faculties to clear the psyche of unwanted imprints by replacing them with more powerful images of what we want. And we must learn to trust the psyche to manifest whatever we ask of it by suggestion, no matter how large or trivial.

Chapter Eight

THE TRANSFORMATIONAL PROCESS

The more conscious we become of the way our psyches function, the more we realize that in order to reflect and radiate the Light represented by the real Self, we must first cleanse and purify our psyches. The need for this kind of purification of the psyche is one of the central teachings of the Wisdom Tradition. That is because as long as there is any content in our private worlds or our psyches that remains unconscious or unknown to us, that content will pull us back into identification with group realities and into affinities with other personalities.

"Affinities" are frequency registrations that cause us to synchronize our functional activities with another or others, usually unconsciously. When affinities are "positive," we act, feel, and think like others, not because we have consciously chosen to do so, but because our psyches are unconsciously reflecting (and thus re-creating) the realities those persons represent.

If the affinities are "negative," we act, feel and think *in reaction to* those in our acquaintance whom we do *not* like. By our reactions we hope to diminish the influence of these others by creating a reality contrary to theirs. Nevertheless, we remain caught in their frequencies as long as we are reacting to them, for the reality we create is determined by theirs, even if we are reflecting a polar opposite expression.

If we want to function consciously and to express through our personalities the Light registered in the real Self, then we must bring into consciousness the entire content of both our private worlds and our psyches and sort through it, letting go of all that is not in harmony with the higher frequencies we have begun to register and retaining only what is. Then when we turn the mirror of the psyche to the real Self it will be able to reflect without distortion the pattern of the real Self.

It is possible to do much of your private world "housecleaning" by yourself, just by paying attention to your thoughts, your opinions, your judgments, your values, and your interpretations. As you examine them in the light of what is actually transpiring in energy, you must also see how they measure up with your highest values.

Bringing things up from the unconscious into the light of consciousness can be more difficult, and often it is helpful to enlist the help of a counselor or therapist when you find yourself unable to work through a difficulty in your life.

The process of sorting and cleansing, letting go of what no longer serves you, is called the transformational process. It is very intense during the early period after we open to real Self frequency registration, and it continues each time we register a still higher frequency and discover as a result that some other pattern in the personality is no longer in harmony and must be released.

We do not usually undertake the transformational process by conscious choice. Often we are thrown into it by a life event that makes us realize that we are stuck.

Sometimes we develop a physical illness that forces us to stop and consider the way we have been living our lives. Sometimes we are thrown into emotional turmoil due to a relationship that is disrupted by conflict, separation, or death. Sometimes we experience a crisis of meaning and our old ways of making sense of our lives no longer work for us. These and other life circumstances create the kind of pressure that causes us to enter into the transformational process.

If we listen inwardly, we will be guided to and through such times by the voice of the real Self, which speaks to us through intuition or inner guidance. There will be times when we will focus on the cleansing and refining of the physical body through fasting and careful regulation of our diets. At other times, we will go into therapy to resolve and release emotional issues. At still other times, we will immerse ourselves in intense study in order to clear out and reorganize our private worlds and to learn new mental patterns that reflect the natural order of the energy world.

The timing of such transformational work is very individual. It has no given sequential order. And often we repeat aspects of it on a new turn of the spiral of our unfolding. People come into our lives at crucial turning points to guide us through a segment of the transformational process. Then they or we move on and we contact new influences to bring us to our next stage of change.

Sometimes we will be drawn into a relationship that brings into consciousness patterns in our psyche of which we have been unaware. The particular chemistry of the interactions with that individual may "bring out the worst in us." What a gift! That makes it easy for us to see what needs to be released and transformed if we are to continue our growth into identification with the real Self.

How Long Does This Transformational Process Take?

We do not complete any of the phases of the awakening process in a single lifetime, nor do we move through them in perfect sequential order. Rather, as we make strides into and through the various phases in a given lifetime, we build into our increasingly autonomous energy field life skills and qualities of being that are carried over from lifetime to lifetime.

While still in a state of relative unconsciousness in the early stages of each earth life, the personality is able to profit through intuition from the knowing-through-experience already acquired by the real Self. Intuition is wisdom held as real-Self knowing, available to the personality before it consciously knows (Third Eye Center functioning) *that* it knows and *how* it knows. Thus, in a given lifetime we may have the wisdom not to develop certain characteristics, group identities, and affinities, because of an intuitive sense of what is or is not in harmony for us. This is quite different from a rational judgment of what is right or wrong, for it is based solely on the real Self's knowing of what experiences it needs for its further development, and what experiences it does *not* need because they would be repetitious. What each autonomous field needs for its unfoldment will differ from what every other individualizing unit of consciousness needs.

Similarly, the length and depth of the transformational process depends on the learning and growing each individual has undergone in the past. When we have developed to the extent that we consciously embrace the process of transformation, it is like a harvest. All the qualities and faculties the psyche has developed are gathered into conscious awareness. The fruits of learning are gleaned and duly registered as real-Self **knowing gained through experience**. The rest – the chaff – is thrown away or burned in the purifying fire of consciousness (called the Christos, the Kundalini force, or the baptism of fire). The ground of our being is thus cleared for the new.

The end result of the transformational process is that the psyche becomes a clear reflection of the autonomous field, the real Self. The pattern of the autonomous field has been built with the energy substance of conscious knowing developed in the experiences we call life. The psyche thus becomes a vehicle through which real-Self knowing – the truth of one's own being—can be brought into form, given expression, and lived out. Then, in the natural order of things, what we know must be shared with others functioning with less conscious awareness in and through their personalities. This is our version of scattering seeds of new beginning. *The psyche becomes a totally responsive instrument for Self-expression and for service to others.*

How Can We Fuel The Transformational Process In Ourselves?

One of the most important discoveries during this second phase of awakening is **conscious breathing**. Conscious breathing serves very important functions in the process of awakening.

First, it enables us to bring into conscious awareness (to register in Third Eye Chakra frequencies) the entire content of our psyches. Thus, *conscious breathing facilitates the transformational process and the reclamation of wisdom* acquired by the real Self as fruits of learning through other personality expressions as mentioned above.

Second, *conscious breathing acts as a transformer*. When we take in energy waves sent forth from other personalities with private world information loaded onto them, we are able to draw those energies into the cleansing breath of consciousness, to free them of all private world information or data loaded on by the sender, and to lift them to a higher frequency where they can be released in clarity and freedom, giving new life to Self as well as to the one who first sent the energies forth.

Third, *conscious breathing makes it possible to guide and direct the flow of forces through the five energy centers*. As we direct energy through the chakras, we increase the life-charge in our field. Gradually we condition psyche and body to receive and transmit more refined (higher) frequency energy. We become more powerful in our self-expression.

Finally, *conscious breathing helps us to recognize the presence of the real Self.* The physical breath is the functional link between the psyche and the real Self. By learning to breathe consciously – that is, to synchronize one's conscious awareness with the breath flow – we become conscious of how this connection is sustained. The Life Force courses through our energy fields, charging and recharging them with life. On the physical level the Life Force provides the energy with which our bodies perform all their functions and with which we move and express ourselves. The breath is the flow of that Force as it is experienced by the physical senses.

Simultaneous with the physical breath there is a flow of force through the psyche. The Life Force in the psyche enables us to feel and think, and to know ourselves consciously. We experience a rush of energy that makes us feel more personally alive and present.

On the level of the real Self, the Life Force, drawn in and released in a parallel and simultaneous flow with the physical breath, awakens direct knowing and the experience of union with all that is. On the level of real Self, the Life Force is also known as the Christos Power. It awakens us to a new level of reality.

How Can We Learn To Breathe Consciously?

Begin with the simple exercise of following the physical breath with conscious awareness. Notice the in-breath and the out-breath. Then gradually begin to slow the breath down and deepen it by drawing in more air. Be sure you expand your breath from the diaphragm, imagining that you are filling the lungs from the bottom up, as a jar fills when water is poured into it. Balance the in-breath and the out-breath by counting as you inhale and as you exhale. Practice this simple deep breath five or ten minutes each morning until it becomes natural. Then set the intention to breathe that way throughout the day.

During most of the day you will forget about your breathing, but when you get into a difficult situation, turn your attention to it. Often you will feel "stuck" and it may seem that you have completely stopped breathing. If you take time for one or two deep breaths, you will unblock your Life Force and get it flowing freely again. You will find you can think more clearly and make better choices about how to respond.

Gradually you will learn to guide and direct the flow of the Life Force through your physical body. Remember that energy follows your attention, so as you breathe in, hold your attention on the place in the body where there is pain, congestion, or discomfort. As you breathe in consciously and direct the energy in this way, with your attention, you will find that the Life Force quickens, heals, and regenerates the body through the release of Generative Chakra energies.

Through this practice of conscious breathing and directing the energy in the physical body, you will gradually expand your consciousness to include the psyche. By holding your attention focused in the part of the body that corresponds to each chakra, you can consciously direct the flow of the forces through the Solar Plexus, Heart, Throat, and Third Eye Chakras, thus quickening the personality expression, making it malleable, vital, enthusiastic, and coherent.

By learning to guide, direct, channel, and release the Life Force in the body and psyche you prepare yourself for conscious identification with the real Self. When the Life Force is released into our consciousness on the real-Self level we are empowered in an entirely new way. For many centuries in many traditions, the Force on that level has been called the Christos, the Mind of Christ, the Christ Power, the Power of the Holy Spirit, or the Kundalini.

All three levels can be coordinated with the use of an integrative focus. On the in-breath, mentally say, "I breathe in Light." Visualize Light descending through the Crown Center just above the head and filling your entire field with Light. Then, as you exhale, silently affirm, "I breathe out Love." Visualize a beautiful pink (or green) light radiating out spherically from your Heart Center and expanding to encompass all within the range of your consciousness.

Another way to practice an integrative focus is first to inwardly invite the Light to descend as you inhale. Visualize it pouring down into your energy field, bringing it to life. Second, invite the Light to take form in you as you hold your breath and infuse your whole field with it. Third, on the exhale invite the Light to expand into your world, both through your actions and through Its own radiation.

As you practice in these ways, you will begin to experience the power of the Christos working within you. You will remember what you knew in former lifetimes, that you are the real Self in whom the Christos lives and works.

When the Christos Force is consciously released in us, we pass into the third phase of the process of awakening.

Chapter Nine

PHASE THREE OF THE AWAKENING: SHIFTING IDENTITY TO THE REAL SELF

Phase three constitutes the culmination of the process of awakening on the human level. The plant of consciousness of Self comes to full growth, flowers, puts forth fruit, and drops the seeds of a new beginning. The real Self becomes entirely autonomous. In phase three of the awakening, we no longer identify with or feel dependent on any human group. As the individualized real Self we function as independent units, consciously, willingly, and eagerly assuming and fulfilling our place in the fabric of the cosmos. Having become conscious of ourselves as cells in the whole cosmic body, we are now ready to unfold into conscious knowledge of the Whole, and we turn to the Christos energy field for our affiliation and guidance. Thus, having arrived at the end of the individualizing process, we are at the beginning of a process of conscious synthesis with the Whole.

During the third phase of the process of awakening, we cease to be identified with the body or the psyche. We become totally identified with the real Self. Instead of saying, "I am the body," or, "I am this personality," we now simply affirm, "I AM." It is in this phase that we actually awaken from the life dream.

The individualizing field becomes entirely autonomous when the two remaining energy centers come into full consciousness. These two chakras represent the energy polarities of the real Self. The Sacral Chakra represents the yin polarity of the autonomous field. When the frequencies of this chakra are registered in consciousness, we know *potential* – the potential to be and do anything and everything. The Crown Chakra represents the opposite, or yang polarity. When the frequencies of the Crown register in consciousness we know *power* – power to be conscious; power to express ourselves; power to create, to generate, at will. When the energies of the Crown and Sacral Chakras unite, the power and potential are released through the Heart Center as the Christos. When identification with the Christos energy is complete, the individual awakens fully to Self as "I AM," an essential part of the Whole.

Does The Third Phase Of The Awakening Happen All Of A Sudden?

For the majority of humans, this third phase in the process of awakening does not occur all at once. Like the first two phases, the awakening to the Christos will come in stages. Many of us receive vivid glimpses of a new reality when small bursts of the Christos Force are released into our fields. Those moments are life changing. What we glimpse is so radically different from the world as we perceive it in our objective state of consciousness that we know we will never be the same again. We are like infants born into a new body but not yet able to function very well in it. We continue the process of phase two while taking our baby steps into phase three.

With or without glimpses, gradual growth into identification with the real Self is organic and natural. If we were to register the full power of the Sacral and Crown Chakras while we are still identified with the personality, we might think that the personality has access to all power and all potential. The Christos energy would then get pulled down in frequency and the psyche and body would cause distortion of both perception and functioning. If the Christ Force were released in full power while we are still identified with our private worlds, we would perceive our values as right for all persons. Righteous dictators would emerge as a result.

When the Christos power is taken into a state of objective identification, which is a fairly common occurrence, the personality thinks it and it alone is enlightened. The statement of "I AM" is confused in the world of polar opposites to mean, "I AM, but you are not." An egotism results which leads either to a fanatical assertion of one personality over others, or to what we call "madness" – dissociation on the part of the "illumined" one from the communal reality. We often read about such individuals in the newspaper or see them on the streets. They wander about, declaring themselves to be prophets, or asserting that God has spoken to them or directed them to take certain actions. Many times they end up in mental institutions or in prison. Anyone who has entered this third phase of awakening is aware of these dangers of distortion.

In past expressions of the Wisdom Tradition, aspirants were put through rigorous training to prepare body and psyche to be vehicles for the expression of the Christos. It was understood that the faculties of the Higher

Triad, Will, Intuition, and Reason, could only function through the personality after the Lower Quaternary of physical, etheric, emotional and mental bodies were cleansed of inharmonious attributes and qualities and brought into alignment with the truths as taught in the Sacred Science.

Today many of us go through this transformational process without the guidance of initiates of the Wisdom, as mentioned at the end of our discussion of phase two of the awakening.

How Is The Body Refined?

Refinement of the physical body occurs over time and in stages. Generally speaking, it begins with some form of dietary regulation to free the psyche from any addictions that have taken root in the body. This involves working with both Generative and Solar Plexus Chakra energies. Sometimes the process includes fasting, sometimes eating only vegetarian foods, sometimes giving up such things as sugar, coffee, alcohol, tobacco, and other drugs, both prescription and recreational. We take on such dietary restrictions in response to an inner urge and the regimen lasts only as long as the inner Self requires. Once this physical cleansing process is complete, a deeper refinement begins.

The second phase of the physical transmutation can be likened to rewiring the electricity in a house so that more appliances, and of higher voltage, can be used without blowing the circuits. In a similar way, the body needs to be prepared to register and transmit higher frequency energies at greater amperage. In Yoga, the body is prepared for these changes by the use of asanas, postures and positions designed to stimulate certain glands and energy flows in the body.

Those who do not practice Yoga will find that the real Self will undertake this stage of the transmutation in its own time. All we have to do is to trust the process. We must not let the objective mind convince us that something is organically wrong when the symptoms of the rewiring occur. This process takes place in the etheric body rather than the physical, but as the physical body adjusts to reflect the changes, the sensations can be painful. They will be less painful if the body has been physically cleansed first and if we understand that there is nothing wrong with the body. It is simply reflecting a process going on in the etheric body that will, in the long run, make us stronger.

Through this process, subtle changes in the body are brought about, both chemically and structurally. It is very helpful to have a live human being to consult at such times, someone who has gone through the process and understands it through experience. This is a function a teacher would ordinarily fulfill, but a companion in the Great Work can also serve. Such companions can be found through study groups, or by asking within for a companion and trusting the psyche to find one for you.

Finally we awaken to the awareness that the Will has been buried in the body, working through the muscles on all levels. Through focused breathing exercises, we learn how to direct nerve currents moving through the body so we can express the Will consciously.

How Are The Emotions Refined?

In a similar fashion, our emotional life needs to be cleansed and refined in both the Solar Plexus and the Heart Centers. The first phase is to recognize the addictions and affinities that keep us bound in relationships. If we love some people too much, having put them at the center of our lives, we are not free to do the Great Work. For example, fears about how those people will feel or what they will think of our choices make it difficult for us to sense and follow inner guidance from the real Self. Likewise, if we hate, feel antagonistic toward, or get irritated by someone, we are not free. Such persons tug at our awareness and influence our decision-making in subtle if not obvious ways.

Getting free of such strong emotional attachments is not easy. Many who are on the spiritual path rebel at the very idea, fearing that they will become cold and unfeeling as a result. Actually, the reverse is true. When we free ourselves from particular affinities, both positive and negative, and especially from addictive relationships (those to which we cannot say "no"), we find that we are able to love other persons for *who they are,* perhaps for the very first time. Until then, we love others for what we need from them, not for who they are.

Which brings us to the Heart Center. Often we discover repressed grief that needs to be released before we can begin to love unconditionally and universally. This might be personal grief, but more often it is universal grief for all the pain and sorrow in the world, which we register daily but usually do not allow ourselves to feel and release. Also we may find that we have fears in the Heart Center that we have never recognized. Those fears need to be faced, felt, and released, no matter what their nature.

Once we have cleared the Solar Plexus and Heart Centers, we can begin to recalibrate our feeling registry so that we are attuned to the real Self within. This illumines our sense of morality so that we want to do the right thing in each circumstance according to our inner

Light, not because of group mores or expectations. In addition, we begin to find that our intuition, which is the registry of the "voice" of the real Self, grows steadily stronger. We are no longer dependent on other people or outer facts to give us guidance. A flawless sense of inner direction takes over.

Does The Mind Have To Be Cleared Of Negative Thoughts?

The objective mind needs to be brought into alignment with the Wisdom Teachings. This means clearing out many old beliefs, admonitions, words of advice, and opinions that were registered and developed in our early years and that are clear contradictions of truth as we are now coming to know it. As we do this work, we will find ourselves out of step with old friends and with groups to which we have belonged for years, and we must be prepared to move on, letting go of those associations.

Reason is understood in the Wisdom to be the ability to use the objective mind to examine experience in the Light of the truth as taught in the Sacred Science. Initiates develop Reason by a profound study and constant application of the Sacred Science, which teaches them to place themselves in conscious relation to the hidden forces of the universe.

Things that are understood by the masses to be tragic (like death), we come to see as natural and liberating. Other things thought to be essential (such as material possessions, good reputations, outstanding positions of responsibility) we will consider secondary at best, and sometimes even detrimental to spiritual development.

As we learn to understand that the objective mind is only a mirror that captures reflections of the real and the true, we will want to polish that mirror and hold it steady so that we can find the words to express with conviction and precision the truths we are coming to know.

Will These Cleansings Release The Latent Powers Of Our Divinity?

When we are able to bring expressions of the higher faculties of Will (activated through the body), Intuition (sensed through the cleansed emotional body), and Reason (expressed through a polished objective mind) into complete agreement with our perception of truth, then we can begin to develop latent faculties, or powers, to unlimited degrees. These latent powers (such as true clairvoyance, healing, bi-location, conscious manifestation, and many others) are often thought to be out of our reach. However, they can be developed if we have prepared our vehicles of expression through these disciplines of the process of initiation during the second and third phases of awakening. Sometimes they are even spontaneously released.

What Are Some Of The Beginning Steps In Developing Those Latent Powers?

During the process of awakening we learn that energy follows our attention and that mental patterns give form to energy substance. Therefore, by learning to concentrate and hold our attention steady, we can manifest what we hold as a clear image in the polished mirror of the mind.

We also learn the importance of purpose, or intention. Unless we are conscious of what we want to bring into being, we will continue to serve unconscious impulses and urges from the group psyches with which we are or have been identified. Once we have clarified our purpose, however, and the steps that will move us toward the fulfillment of that purpose (objectives), we can make conscious choices about what urges to manifest and begin to set something new into motion. We can be creative and co-creative through activities that are motivated by sharply defined objectives.

In addition, the cleansing of the psyche arouses our subtle senses. These are like the physical senses, but they enable us to register the frequencies of the higher worlds as described by the Sacred Science and to communicate with angels and archangels, not on a psychic level, but directly in the higher frequencies.

When Will, Intuition, and Reason are highly developed, direct spiritual perception of the energy world itself begins to open. This is the highest accomplishment, and it occurs by transforming the lowest or grossest frequency level of the manifested being, namely the body, so that we can see the unseeable and know the unknowable.[15] Very few achieve this level of initiation because of how difficult it is, but it is worth aspiring toward.

In the realm of the psyche, *images* of the energy world predominate, and those images are different for different persons and different groups. However, those who awaken to the energy world find themselves living in *one common reality*. This is the real world of clear perception, of knowing without thinking. It is the Noetic Mind

---

[15] For some samples of historical personages who began to taste of such higher forms of perception, read *Cosmic Consciousness,* by Maurice Bucke, New York: E. P. Dutton & Co., 1901, and Appendix One of *Four Paths to Union,* by Mariamne Paulus, Scottsdale, AZ: Teleos Imprint, 2001.

Figure 4: THE AUTONOMOUS FIELD (REAL SELF)

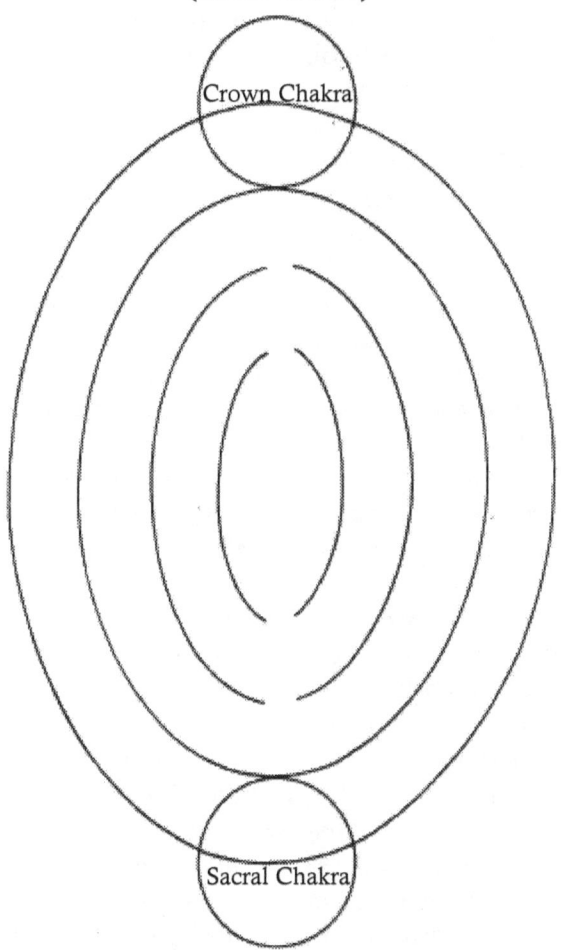

When the Crown and Sacral Chakras are brought into consciousness, the Autonomous Field sustains the lines of force on which the personality forms according to its perfect pattern. All sense of separation between the personality and the real Self disappears.

level, which has been called Christ Consciousness in the Western tradition of the Wisdom.

Here is an example of one whose latent powers were opening. In his book *Vitvan: An American Master,*[16] Richard Satriano writes:

> *[Vitvan] was undergoing an awesome orientation to new levels of perception and awareness. He had no teacher, nor even any reliable books to explain his experiences. His background provided no references. The sweeping changes in his psychological functioning might well have caused lesser men to doubt their sanity. But his stubborn practicality allowed him to accept all such phenomena as natural and providential to his development.*
>
> *"I believed," [Vitvan] said, "that God alone was my mentor. When I could not understand the nature of things experienced, I prayed in simple faith: 'The Lord is my shepherd...'"*
>
> *He often experimented with the extensional faculties he was newly discovering. One such instance is described in his superb work,* The Christos.[17]
>
> *"On the trails in the evening I would oft-times select a young evergreen or other tree and sit down a short distance from it. I would withhold thoughts from forming a concept – that is, thing, object, green, tree, etc. – and I would also restrain thoughts from wandering off into other remembrances. After a few months of this practice, flickers of what looked like flame began to appear here and there, in and out of the tree. As time passed, with more opportunities to practice, these flickers of flame*

---

[16] Baker, NV: School of the Natural Order, 1977, pages 15-17.
[17] By Vitvan. Baker, NV: School of the Natural Order, 1951.

became more steady, until they enveloped the whole tree. As this envelopment proceeded, I lost the ability to see an object – that is, what we call a tree – and I knew with intuitive certainty that I was seeing the real. I learned in time to transfer this seeing at will from the objective level to the real in regard to any 'thing' or 'object.' I could only assume that for reasons unknown to myself I was able to function in two worlds. I accepted the fact with gratitude."

Then, as footnote to the staying power of his self-certainty, he adds, "*Not until years later did I realize I was able to see the One world in two distinct ways: as it appears in Light's structure and as it is crystallized into pictures of things and objects that we see and experience. This is the phenomenal world that our senses abstract from the real – a private world having no existence outside of our own mental formulation.*"

This occurrence of seeing the archetypal structures of objects – i.e., the dynamic energy patterns of Light that describe objective reality and from which we perceive our phenomenal world –has been witnessed by seer and initiate alike, from Moses and the burning bush to Carlos Castaneda and his experience of 'stopping the world' and 'seeing.' [Journey to Ixtlan, chapter 19, "Stopping the World."] The faculty to perceive on this level is a natural development in self-unfoldment. But the how's and why's of it are seldom explained by the authors who write accounts of it. One will find, however, a detailed description of the phenomena, and a precise methodology to attain it, in Vitvan's The Christos.

How Long Does This Initiation, Or Process Of Awakening, Take?

Initiation is a very slow transformational process, a metamorphosis that takes place over many months, years, and lifetimes. Gradually our original sense of self is transformed so that it can serve on higher levels. This is what is meant in the Bible by the death of the old self and birth of the new self. Our psyches are able to serve the real Self. All desire for things and objects has been burned away, through pursuit and fulfillment of the desires, or through release of them when we find that they cannot be fulfilled or that their fulfillment leaves us still unsatisfied. We let go of all resistance, and surrender completely to the truth.

Achieving this level of development is the aim of the process of initiation. The Wisdom Teachings say that when we develop direct spiritual perception we achieve immortality. That is, we are freed from the cyclic process called reincarnation. We will take on bodies again only if it serves the larger purpose of completing the creating process set in motion by the Original One.

What Would It Be Like To Be Immortal?

In phase three of the awakening, we come to know the real Self as the Power-To-Be-Conscious. That power is not bound by time and space. Thus we are able at will to leave both the body and the psyche, recognizing both for what they are: vehicles of expression. In our objective state of consciousness we get in and out of vehicles of transportation (cars, planes, trucks, tractors, ski-mobiles) at will, according to circumstances and our intention or need. We also pick up and use instruments of communication (letters, telephones, wireless, cables, satellites, computers) at will. In a similar way, when we are identified with the real Self we are able to take on a body and a personality at will, and to leave off one or both at will, according to circumstances and intention.

People have tastes of this ability to leave their bodies in what are called "out of the body" experiences. For example, some who have been in severe automobile or plane accidents report afterwards that they could look down and see their bodies in the wrecked vehicle. Sometimes people have a similar experience when they are under anesthesia. However, in most instances these people do not leave their bodies consciously; they simply "find themselves" looking down at their bodies.[18]

Fully individualized Beings are able to leave not only their bodies but also their personalities at will. For examples of these extraordinary powers that come in the third phase of awakening, read *Autobiography of a Yogi*, by Paramahansa Yogananda,[19] *Masters of the Far East (Vols. 1-6)*, by Baird T. Spalding,[20] *Meetings with Remarkable Men*, by G. I. Gurdjieff,[21] and others.[22]

When we are totally identified with the real Self we can function effectively and freely through a personality, and yet in no way be identified with it. We *know* we are *not* the personality, and thus we can change families, reli-

---

[18] The Monroe Institute teaches people conscious projection of the psyche out of the body. The Monroe Institute, 62 Roberts Mountain Road, Faber, VA 22938. www.monroeinstitute.org/
[19] Los Angeles: Self-Realization Fellowship, 1969.
[20] Marina del Rey, CA: De Vorss & Co., 1924, 1927, 1935, 1948, 1955, 1996.
[21] New York: Penguin Arkana Books, 1985.
[22] Other books to explore: *Kundalini: The Evolutionary Energy in*

gions, ethnic or racial groups, nationalities and cultures without any difficulty. We can assume a new personal identity without any confusion regarding the "I AM."

In this fully individualized state, we embrace in consciousness all facets of the unfolding consciousness, but we no longer emerge *from a group* when assuming a body and a personality. Instead, we generate with the Christos Power those vehicles needed for functioning. Thus, from the beginning of a life cycle, the body and personality reflect the perfect pattern held in the autonomous field. No transformation is needed since no affinities are established and no patterns from human groups are reflected. We become living examples of the power and clarity of conscious co-creators.

When we are totally identified with the real Self we are forever youthful, vital, dynamic, flexible and filled with power. We have become more than human. We have become Christed ones, fully awakened. Ahead of us lies the wondrous adventure of synthesizing in our consciousness all that is represented by the Original One.

That is the promise that is held before us. It is based on the experience of those who have gone before us and who light the way for us as we go through the process of

---

Man, by Gopi Krishna, Berkeley, CA: Shambala, 1971; *Modern Mystics,* by Sir Francis Younghusband, New York: Books for Libraries Press, Inc., 1967; *Vitvan: An American Master,* by Richard Satriano, Baker, NV: School of the Natural Order, 1977; *The Common Experience,* by J. M. Cohen and J-F. Phipps, Los Angeles: J. P. Tarcher, 1979; *Higher Creativity: Liberating the Unconscious for Breakthrough Insights,* by Willis Harman and Howard Rheingold, Los Angeles: J. P. Tarcher, 1984; *Coming Home: The Experience of Enlightenment in Sacred Traditions,* by Lex Hixon, Los Angeles: J. P. Tarcher, 1978.

awakening. May you find your way to direct perception of the truth, integrate what you come to know into your everyday living, and come to the full flowering of your Being so that you know the joy of living in consciousness of the real Self.

Works Cited:
Brunton, Paul. *A Search in Secret India*. New York: Samuel Weiser, Inc., 1970.
Hodson, Geoffrey. *Hidden Wisdom in the Holy Bible*, Vol. I. Wheaton, IL: Quest Books, 1993.
Knight, Gareth. *Esoteric Training In Everyday Life*. Oceanside, CA: Sun Chalice Books, 2001.
Kybalion, The. By Three Initiates. Chicago: Yogi Publication Society, 1936.
Spalding, Baird T. *Life and Teachings of the Masters of the Far East, Vol II*. Los Angeles: DeVorss Books, 1927/72.

GLOSSARY

The definitions given are in accordance with the usage in this book and may vary somewhat from usage in other contexts.

ABSTRACTING – forming an image in the psyche, with its qualities and characteristics, by mental separation from the particular situation, event, or object.

AFFINITY – resonance or synchronization of functional activities with another, or others, usually unconsciously; sympathetic vibration with another or others, or antipathetic vibration causing reactions to or against another.

ARCHETYPE – an original pattern from which all other things of the same kind are made; a universal, perfect pattern.

ASANA – a posture or position designed to stimulate certain glands and energy flows in the body (Sanskrit).

ASTRAL: the substance of which the psyche is made and in which emotions and thoughts take form.

ASTRAL WORLD – a realm of higher frequencies than can be registered by the physical senses, often called the psychic world.

AUTONOMOUS FIELD – the field of a fully individualized human whose consciousness is centered in oneness and who is no longer divided into various senses of self; one who is no longer dependent on identification with human groups but is oriented to the Christos; also called the Noetic Mind, because the individual functions from knowing rather than sensing. (See also, Christos and Spirit.)

BEINGS – when capitalized, entities that are fully individualized and therefore autonomous, living in the eternal present.

CHAKRA – literally (in the Sanskrit) a wheel: a vortex of energy corresponding to a given wave frequency band; a focal point for the transformation of cosmic energies so that they can be used by humans in the Great Work.

CHRISTOS – the dynamic force that awakens within each of us, motivating us to drop our identification with the psyche and to reorient ourselves to the cosmic process and our rightful place within it; the state of consciousness in which a human comes to know oneness with Self and with the cosmos. (See also, Autonomous Field and Spirit.)

ENLIGHTENED – one who knows the real Self and is identified with it is called enlightened; living in Light's Regions.

ETHERIC – an energy substance finer and higher in frequency than the physical body, that mediates between the psyche and the body; sometimes referred to as the etheric double of the physical body.

GREAT MOTHER – the yin or feminine polarity of the creating power that brings everything into being.

GREAT WORK – the purpose of human life, namely, to bring into consciousness the Primal Will that motivates the cosmic process and to cooperate consciously with that Will.

IDENTIFY WITH – to establish one's identity through association with; to know oneself as. (For example, to be identified with the body is to know "I am this body," or even, "this body is what I am.")

INDIVIDUALIZING PROCESS – the process by which humans become whole, indivisible in their consciousness, and identified with the real Self.

INTUITION – wisdom held as real-Self knowing, available to the personality before it consciously knows *that* it knows and *how* it knows.

LIGHT MOTHER – the Great Mother in her virginal state, before she begins to give "birth" to the cosmos.

OBJECTIVE CONSCIOUSNESS, OBJECTIVE MIND – ordinary human consciousness, in which both subject and object are necessary for perception; thus, characterized by duality. The objective mind includes the faculty of intellect as distinguished from emotion or will, the faculty of abstract thinking, the memory, and the capacity for symbolic communication and the use of language. It is used to record, sort out, and give order to experience.

PRIVATE WORLD – the abstracted memory of each individual in which are held the stories we tell ourselves about our life experience, including our opinions, preferences, judgments, values, world views, beliefs, etc.; unique to each individual and unknowable by others.

The Process of Awakening   165

QUICKENING – an arousal of the Christos power within the individual.

REASON – the ability to examine experience in the light of truth as taught in the Sacred Science.

REGISTER – to record in consciousness.

SEERS – Beings with perceptive insight, which is the ability to see things as they are in the Energy World; those who function in the Noetic Mind.

SPIRIT – the highest frequency bands in the developing human being. (See also Autonomous Field and Christos.)

SUBSTANCE – energy, the "stuff" of which the cosmos is made.

SUBCONSCIOUSNESS – consciousness that is below the surface of our awareness; the accumulated experience and wisdom of all that preceded us in the evolutionary process.

SUPERCONSCIOUSNESS – consciousness that is higher in frequency than our current state of consciousness.

THROUGHLINE – the three facets of Self (body, psyche, and spirit) aligned in both intention and function.

WAKING DREAM – the objective state of consciousness.

WILL – with a capital w, the motivating force behind the creating process that brings the cosmos into being; with a small w, the reflection of the Higher Will in each human being.

WISDOM, THE – a body of teachings about the nature of the universe and of human beings, including instruction for how human beings can unfold their potential and awaken to higher consciousness.

YANG – the masculine, or positive (electrical), polarity of energy.

YIN – the feminine, or negative (magnetic), polarity of energy.

INDEX

A
Addictions, 149–51
Affinities, 31, 137, 149–52
Animal consciousness, 57–59
Archetypes, 19
Astral, 84; *See also,* Substance, astral and World, astral
Autonomous fields, 24, 31, 60–61
Awakened, experience of being, 51–55
Awakening
    length of process of, 158
    process of, 35–56
    seeking psychiatrists and, 75–76
Awakenings
    gradual, 46–48
    reluctant, 48–50
    spontaneous, 44–46
    sudden, 39–44

B
Beings, 7, 19
Body, 79-82, 149–50, 153
    Emotional, 24, 27, 78, 80, 150–52, 153
    Etheric, 24, 27, 36, 78
    Mental, 24, 28, 78, 84, 152–53
    Physical, 24, 27, 36, 78
Body and psyche, functioning consciously through, 94–136
Breathing, conscious, 141–145

C

Chakras, 100–29
    Crown, 147
    Generative, 100, 101–08, 149
    Heart, 100, 101, 114–18, 151
    Sacral, 147
    Solar Plexus, 100, 108–14, 149–51
    Third Eye, 100, 122–29, 140, 141
    Throat, 100, 118–22
Christos, 31–32, 96, 141, 143, 145, 146–49, 160
Consciously, learning to function, 94–136
    having what we want, 112–13
    changing feelings of separation, 106–07
    Generative Chakra, 104–06
    Heart Chakra, 117–18
    Solar Plexus Chakra, 110–12
    Third Eye Chakra, 125–129
    Throat Chakra, 118–22
Consciousness
    animal, 57–59
    Christ, 156
    objective, 57–70, esp. 62–64, 67–69
    self, 69–70
Control center, identifying in Self, 95–96

D

Divine Force, 16, 23–24
Divine Science; *See* Sacred Science
Divinity, 24, 153
Dreams, 59–67, 61–62, 64–67

E

Emotions, 150–52
Energy centers; *See* Chakras
Energy fields
    human, 100–02
    group, 30–31

Energy world, 12–13, 18, 26–31, 62–64, 66–67, 97–100, 104–06, 108–11, 116–117, 125 –27, 154
Etheric; *See* Body, etheric

F
Feelings, 80–82, 106–07
Fields, energy
    autonomous, 60–61
    group, 30-31
First principle, 15, 24
Force; *See* God force and Yang force
Four worlds, 17-19

G
General Semantics, 66
Generative Chakra, 100, 102–108, 149
God
    attributes of, 18, 20
    separate from, 26
    made in image of, 24–25
    Wisdom teachings about, 15–17
Great Mother, 67
Great Work, 26-27, 151

H
Heart Chakra, 100, 102, 114–18, 151
Hermetic Principles, 21-23, 35
Hope for humans, 69–70
Human energy fields, structure of, 100–02
Human life, purpose of, 26–30
Human sleep states, 57–70
Humanity, Wisdom Teachings about, 23–24
Humans
    made in image of God, 24–25
    hope for, 69–70
    laws and principles that apply to, 30–32
    true structure of, 78–79, 100–02

I
Identity, shifting to real self, 146–61
Illusions, 64–66
Immortal, being, 158–61
Initiation, 32, 153, 158
Intuition, 95, 140, 153, 154

K

L
Latent powers, 153–157
Laws and principles, 21–23, 30–32
Life Force, 143–45
Light Mother, 19
Love principles, 107, 113, 115, 122, 125, 127, 129

M
Maya, 26, 51
Mind
    clearing of negative thoughts, 152–53
    Noetic, 32
    objective, *See* Objective consciousness
Mother principle, 15

N
Nature, humans as part of, 25–26, 35
Negative thoughts, clearing mind of, 152–53
Noetic Mind/Self, 32, 96

O
Objective consciousness/mind, 62–4, 67–9, 106–07, 152–53, 159
Original One, 15–20, 23–26, 30–32, 158, 160

P
Past-life recalls, 29–30
Personality, 36–38, 71–91, 72–74, 82–84

Physical body, consciousness and identification with, 57–70
Principle
    Creating, 15
    Father, 15
    First, 15, 24
    Hermetic, 21–23, 35
    Love, 107, 113, 115, 122, 125, 127, 129
    Mother, 15
Private worlds, 66–67, 85–90, 90–92, 92–93, 97–102, 108–12, 115–16, 121, 125–29, 137–39
Psyches, 28
    functioning by reflection, 129–133
    functioning by suggestion, 133–136
    structure of/Chakras in, 100–131
    transforming the, 137–45
Psychotherapists, 75–76

Q
Quaternary, lower, 24, 26, 78, 100, 149
Quest, the, 3–4

R
Real self, shifting identity to, 146–61
Reason, 153–54
Reincarnation, 29

S
Sacred Science, 14–32
Self
    real, 76, 95–96, 142–44, 146
    control center in, 95–96
    shifting identity to real, 147–161
Self-consciousness differing from animal consciousness, 57–59
Seven Rays, the, 17-18, 24
Sleep states, human, 57–70
Solar Plexus Chakra, 100, 108–14, 149–51

Substance, 18
    Astral, 27-28, 36, 84
    Light, 18
Symbolism, 10-11

T
Teachings, Wisdom, 7–13
Therapists: *See* Psychotherapist
Third Eye Chakra/Center, 100, 122–29, 140, 141

Thoughts, 84–85, 152–53
Throat Chakra, 100, 118–22
Transformational process, 137–45
    fueling in ourselves, 141–43
    learning to breathe consciously, 143–45
    length of, 140–41
Triad, higher, 24, 28, 31, 100, 148–49
Trinity, 15
Triune, 16, 24

U
Unfolding, pattern of, 38–39
Universal laws and principles, 21–23
Universe, structure of, 17–20

W
Waking dreams, 59–67, 61–62, 64–67
Will, 153–54
Wisdom Teachings, 7–13
    finding, 8–9
    in the West, 9–10
    status today, 12
World
    astral/Formation, 19, 20
    causal/Divine Emanation, 18–20
    material/Matter, 19, 20
    mental/Creation, 19, 20

Mother, 19
Worlds
　　　energy, 12–13, 18, 26–31, 62–64, 66–67, 97–100, 104–06,
　　　　　108–11, 116–117, 125 –27, 154
　　　private, 66–67, 85–90, 90–92, 92–93, 97–102, 108–12,
　　　　　115–16, 121, 125–29, 137–39
　　　four, 18-20

Y
Yang, 15
Yang force, 25
Yin, 15
Yin Substance, 25

www.ingramcontent.com/pod-product-compliance
Lightning Source LLC
Chambersburg PA
CBHW031247290426
44109CB00012B/473